more pra

Stronger Than Fear

"In his elegy for W.B. Yeats, Auden famously avowed that 'poetry makes nothing happen.' Yet in the very same stanza, he went on to define the art as 'a *way* of happening' (italics mine). In that single word 'way' resides the genius of *Stronger Than Fear*. For all its beautiful diversity, for all the ambitious reach—into ancestry, into history, into hazard and futurity— of the poems gathered here, there is a striking concord and unity of purpose. And that purpose is compassion; and its prospect is of the ways in which compassion, truly voiced, redeems the times in which we live. There is a thrill of humanity in these poems—something to refresh our hopes and to renew our courage."

—Donald Revell

"The poems in *Stronger Than Fear* are the rooms of the world we live in. Their complex truths are artfully arranged to lead us through nerve and redemption, inner and outer. This remarkable anthology enters social and political issues without offering answers. Instead, the poems draw us up to a current of other people's experiences and the tender personal that lies beneath. Through the sinew of crafted lines and the multiplicity of honesties, this collection moves readers toward an unshadowed humanity."

—Lauren Camp

"Rarely has our democracy been more in need of empathy and progressive advocacy than in this present moment. In this striking new anthology, Alexander and Massimilla offer our finest poets of witness in a single potent collection. With each line of this text, our authors are 'making it easier for us to breathe.'"

—Kyle McCord

"During times when society feels in danger of accepting inequities or giving in to despair . . . *Stronger Than Fear* offers consolation, an attentiveness to the world, even a joy that resists defeat. In thematic sections that seek to give voice to wounds and reclaim the stories of history, these poets find the language and community that can give us all courage. Carol Alexander and Stephen Massimilla have gathered poets and poems that remind us that we are more than news headlines sometimes suggest. That humans are capable of great compassion. That poetry can be a vehicle for empowerment. That above all we must never abandon hope; we must notice the world speaking and we must listen."

—Traci Brimhall

"Through poems of empathy, empowerment, and witness, Alexander and Massimilla have compiled an anthology of great aesthetic and political value . . . probing the inequities of wide-ranging social systems. These poems rest together, sometimes uncomfortably, but always in productive tension. . . . Such juxtapositions reveal what Ada Limón, in 'A New National Anthem,' calls the 'unsung third stanza' written into—or beneath, or beside—our most familiar cultural rituals. Curated to unveil these truths, *Stronger Than Fear* prompts us to acknowledge the fraught national histories still very much with us today, and in doing so, encourages us to forge ahead into new and unanticipated social futures."

—John James

Stronger Than Fear

POEMS OF EMPOWERMENT, COMPASSION, AND SOCIAL JUSTICE

EDITED BY

Carol Alexander

&

Stephen Massimilla

涧月亮
CAVE MOON PRESS
YAKIMA 中 WASHINGTON

ISBN: 978-0-9797785-8-2

www.cavemoonpress.com

I am stronger than fear.

*At night our fear is strong . . . but in the morning,
in the light, we find our courage again.*
—Malala Yousafzai

CONTENTS

Carol Alexander and Stephen Massimilla
Introduction xix

Wound Care

Desirée Alvarez
Flor de Corazón 3

Carol Alexander
Blue Calling 4
Shadows That Are 5

Elizabeth Brulé Farrell
Chicken Soup 6

Emily Fragos
Grand Opening 7

Jennifer Franklin
Antigone Visits the Psychiatric Hospital 8

Kate Gale
Wound Care 10

Melissa Hotchkiss
Into the Empty 12

Molly Peacock
Three Young Women 13
Adult Life 14

Patricia Spears Jones
    Shack with Vines   16
    Painkiller   18

Stephen Massimilla
    About Sister   20

Hermine Meinhard
    The Sea   22

Nancy Shiffrin
    Amnesty   26

Maria Terrone
    Your blood was no longer on the stone   28

Not A Small Voice

Elizabeth Alexander
    Amistad   33

Ellen Bass
    Because What We Do Does Not Die   34

Hala Alyan
    Aleppo   35
    Post-Election Morning   38

Reginald Dwayne Betts
    Prison   40
    Sometimes It's Everything   41

Jaswinder Bolina
    Homeland   42

Nancy L. Cook
About Literacy   43

Rosalind Brenner
Women's Music   44

Tina Cane
Rage and Ibuprofen   46

Paola Corso
Arrival   48

Kwame Dawes
Land Ho   51
Talk   52

Toi Derricotte
On the Turning Up of Black
    Unidentified Female Corpses   54
Why I don't write about George Floyd   56

Rita Dove
The Breathing, the Endless News   57

Cornelius Eady
Diabolic   58
Tubman's Rock   59

Ross Gay
A Small Needful Fact   60
Pulled Over in Short Hills, NJ, 8:00 A.M.   61

Maria Mazziotti Gillan
Jayden de Leon, Age 7,
    The Herald News, Wednesday, March 2, 2016   62

Juan Felipe Herrera
Half-Mexican   63

Daniela Gioseffi
Don't Speak the Language of the Enemy   64

Rachel Hadas
Shouldering   66

Brenda Hillman
Crypto-animist Introvert Activism   68

Scott Hightower
A Spontaneous Attack, 2018   69

Jane Hirshfield
Spell to Be Said Against Hatred   72

Major Jackson
In the Eighties We Did the Wop   73

Honorée Fannone Jeffers
An Issue of Mercy #1   74

Yusef Komunyakaa
The African Burial Ground   76
Dead Reckoning I   78

Devi S. Laskar
in praise of the B in Bengali   79

Ada Limón
A New National Anthem   82

Devi S. Laskar
    Taking the Poem from the Poet   84

Maria Lisella
    A Stitch in . . .   85
    They Don't Remember When We Were . . .   86

Stephen Massimilla
    The Workers of Macchu Picchu   88
    The Hitlerian Spring   89

Naomi Shihab Nye
    Two Countries   92

Elise Paschen
    Kitihawa   93

Paisley Rekdal
    有 識: Have Knowledge   94

Sonia Sanchez
    This Is Not a Small Voice   96

Solmaz Sharif
    He, Too   97

Peter Schmitt
    Conversation in Camden County   98

Hilary Sideris
    Questions for the Wanda Coleman Test   100

Mervyn Taylor
    Gum   101
    That One   102
    How the Gun Is Like the Taser   104

Maria Terrone
Afghan Shadows   105

Laura Tohe
Little Sister   106

Natasha Tretheway
Letter Home   108

George Wallace
He Remembers the Sun, the Only Light He Sees   110
For This My Heart the Revolution   112

Marjory Wentworth
One River, One Boat   113

Yvonne
Norman Rockwell and Me   116

Kevin Young
Nightstick [A Mural for Michael Brown]   118

i'd tell you

Kim Addonizio
High Desert, New Mexico   123

Elizabeth Alexander
Blues   124

Ellen Bass
Ode to Invisibility   126

Jaswinder Bolina
Waiting My Turn   128

Grace Cavalieri
Just This   129

Tina Cane
Treatise on My Mouth   130

Ruth Danon
Knowledge Is Power   132

Jennifer Franklin
Biopsy Pantoum   133

Toi Derricotte
I give in to an old desire   134
The Weakness   136

Jane Hirshfield
The Bird Net   138

Tess Gallagher
Sully   139

Jenny Molberg
Epistle from the Hospital for Harassment   142
May the Stars Guide You Safely Home   143

Miller Oberman
"If this was a different kind of story
    I'd tell you about the sea"   146

Paisley Rekdal
Hall of Sea Nettles   148

Lesley Wheeler
Ambitions ~ *Liverpool*   150
Ambitions ~ *Bath*   151

Ellen Rachlin
There Is Already Too Little Difference
    Between Living and Not   152

Lessons In Remembering

Yehuda Amichai
The School Where I Studied   155

Thomas Davison
The Forgotten Faces   156

Lauren Camp
Adult Basic Education   157
Talking Twice   160

Sheryl Clough
Hopes for Novices   162

Sally Dawidoff
The Trace of an Event   164

Lisa Fay
Whittemore Library, Framingham State University   166

Paul Hostovsky
Ninth Grade Vocabulary List   167
Writing Platypuses   168

Major Jackson
Winter   169

Scott Lowery
Shawn   170
Field Trip to Chair City   172

Aimee Nezhukumatathil
On Listening to Your Teacher Take Attendance   174

Naomi Shihab Nye
Separation Wall   176

Tony Reevy
View from the Disputanta School   177

Miller Oberman
This and That at The Frick   178

Catherine Woodard
Gettysburg   180

Jennifer Schneider
Fill in the Blanks   181

Soraya Shalforoosh
Education Has No Borders   184
Asynchronous Learning During
the Pandemic, Week One *with Dylan Yahiaoui*   185

Ancestral Spirits

Joel Allegretti
Lot's Wife   189

Kim Addonizio
Creased Map of the Underworld   190

Desirée Alvarez
Botanical Drawing of Colonialism   192

Ellen Bass
Goat, Cow, Man   194

Lauren Camp
Fairy Tales with Girls   195

Sheryl Clough
What Raven Said   196

Ruth Danon
The Ruins   198

Annie Finch
Brave Women's Amulet   199
Moon For Our Daughters   200

Tess Gallagher
Redwing   201

Rachel Hadas
February 29, 2020   202

Rick Hilles
To Disenchantment   204
To Misunderstanding   206

Jane Hirshfield
In a Former Coal Mine in Silesia   208

Cynthia Hogue
The Bite of the Apple   209

Stephen Massimilla
After the Ritual of Descent   210

Jenny Molberg
    Loving Ophelia Is   212

Ellen Rachlin
    The Invention of Dance   213

Elaine Sexton
    Landscape with Power Lines   214

Laura Tohe
    Kinaaldá   215

Yuyutsu Sharma
    Running Out of Ink   216

Alina Stefanescu
    Aubade with Caged Animals   220
    To Muffin from the Mountainous Molehill   222

Michael Waters
    One Caw   224
    Electric Fence   225

Index of Contributors   227

Notes on Contributors   231

Acknowledgments   259

INTRODUCTION

Poetry never exists in a vacuum. It reflects complex social realities, and poems that point meaningfully to their context can help us to grapple with issues of great relevance and importance. *Stronger Than Fear* presents poems about social justice, empathy, and empowerment—including empowerment through education. While especially relevant to this pivotal historical moment, these works also speak to enduring problems and possibilities of the larger contemporary experience. The poets featured here come from diverse backgrounds, and quite a few face the difficulties of bridging identity and culture. Many of the poems explore the challenge of learning to inhabit the self fully and fiercely despite obstacles and opposition. Shared concerns include racial prejudice, gender bias, xenophobia, the burdens of history, physical and psychological disabilities, manipulation, victimization, humanitarian crises, dehumanization—and the struggle to gain rights and acceptance. Some of the poets find compassion in unlikely places.

In our strife-ridden modern era, addressing, coping with, and raising awareness of the scourges of injustice, inequality, ignorance, and intolerance are critical endeavors. In the interim between the anthology's inception and the present moment, humanity has struggled with a global pandemic and a host of pressing social issues. Contributing dramatically not only to the rate of sickness and death, but likewise to increases in unemployment, hunger, and homelessness, the pandemic has underscored the impact of longstanding inequities in the United States and throughout the world. The plight of refugees and people hoping to gain safety and citizenship, for instance, have been brought into sharper focus. The world has also grappled with the challenges of virtual learning and the needs of students with limited access to computers. Incidents in the US involving police violence and gun violence have been distressingly frequent. Divisiveness, misinformation, conspiratorial thinking, and antidemocratic undercurrents have been increasingly pervasive concerns, compounding these social problems.

Through the voices of teachers, students, and social justice advocates, all of whom are witnesses to human rights struggles, we hope to spotlight ways in which important work goes on. As a beacon of expression, communication, and revelation, poetry can serve not only to portray experiences and convey perceptions and emotions, but also to articulate positions, focus the attention, ask important questions, provoke thought, and redefine our engagement with the role that language plays in our lives.

This book, then, is the fruit of a collaboration seeded in a dialogue about the potency of literature in calling out and, we hope, helping to overcome obstacles to empowerment, social justice, and educational opportunity. Cave Moon is an independent press with a social mission, including, as publisher Doug Johnson stresses, supporting local and global communities with particular needs. Earlier Cave Moon anthologies have addressed food scarcity, domestic violence, and homelessness among military veterans. As part of the Broken Circles anthology project, for example, contributing poets around the country gave readings to raise funds to help stock their local food banks. (San Francisco filled their food bank; New York gave to theirs; contributors around the country all did their part.) In 2018, Johnson turned his attention to education, specifically that of women and girls in underserved populations. In our discussions, we—the publisher and editors—broadened the theme to a social justice perspective encompassing, among its many facets, the classroom, education beyond the written word, and the role of compassion and intuition in daily life in our difficult era.

Some of the poems in this book were collected through open calls, others by way of open-ended solicitation; a number were sought out individually. All of these pieces reflect the input of living authors. Many have never appeared anywhere else; a few are novel adaptations of earlier modern poems. All bear relevance to the overarching themes, some transparently, others more indirectly. Still others bring the mythic or numinous to the themes. Poetry, after all, is a polyvalent art that speaks to our humanity and addresses reality in its luminous particulars. This collection does not lose sight of the mythic, oblique, and numinous in the name of what some might consider more consistently definitive, clear-cut, or absolute because truth is rarely simple and can often be teased out only with the utmost complexity and care.

The proceeds for the anthology will go to The Malala Fund, dedicated to empowering girls around the world through education. Our deep gratitude to Malala Yousafzai, winner of the 2014 Nobel Peace Prize and the World's Children's Prize, for galvanizing dedicated people and communities to fight for progress in parts of the world where education has been denied to many—and for being an inspiration for this book.

—Carol Alexander and Stephen Massimilla

Wound Care

DESIRÉE ALVAREZ

Flor de Corazón

To think her cure may have been growing
all those years in the bark of the tree I planted
in front of her house. In another time the warrior
wove magnolia buds through his armor scented
with cocoa and hung a garland around his neck.
I want to grow magnolia forests for the beetles
and jaguars to climb. In Guatemala they were
harvested for houses, but deep in a secret grove
in Mexican wilderness hides a new species,
neotropical and ancient, known as medicine
to the Zoque People. With mom three years scattered
in the shad field, all I can do this afternoon is listen
to the girl play weather on her ukulele. She ushers
this sheet of water that is now me to the other planet,
the one where no one ever dies, and grief is a plant
as yet undiscovered or banished to the jungle.
See the roots hanging over my bed? They will open
while I'm sleeping, and we will call them orchids.
The moon will rise, we'll name it snow to begin again
from scratch. The heart flower gives great hope.

CAROL ALEXANDER

Blue Calling

Miles from Arizona's creosote and prickly pear
in the autumn scape of leaf over repointed brick
the river's scent reprises all fish scale and fume—
though no field nor tractor in sight,
I've lived where these were daily things,
rudiments of morning's muzzy walk.
No jeweled grasshopper ravages lettuce or hay
but eel-like sewers hum, clotted vowels restrung,
tongue stumbling on the commonest nouns.
Each day I need fewer, just earthen colors and bread
while sometimes a blue cloud dissipates into rain
as it did when I stirred a glass of medicine.
For each cold call, a listener, a deep suspiciousness.
I go off-script to crumble a palm's worth of soil
over one's various dead, taste the citric reflux
of loss not mine. Maybe this anger runs too deep:
what will we do for each other in this century, this land,
a scant supper apart, flag at half-mast flapping
against the home's aluminum side.

CAROL ALEXANDER

Shadows That Are

Against the wall shadows grope, shadows that pin light to stone,
that are carapaces of light when sky negatives to purple black.
Sleeping rough, they fatten for the border crossing
on the fruits of rock vines; uncle who tried to cross too late
waits eternal there. The ivy purposes to warm and shield him.
And shadows are the bodies of Warsaw dreamers lured from bed
by the scent of night-blooming jasmine, by dark eyes under a pergola,
the code of clinking forks. Languages flitter through the rude wall;
to the untutored ear they sound the same, but their blood types differ.
Agents go on drinking vermouth while night bleeds the river
studded with fire opals cold to the tongue. Rooted in shallow soil,
the olive tree of Zion grows against this bitter luxuriance—
peace lifts its shining horn and passes indifferently,
hooves crushing mortar shells while evening prayer,
that dark blossom, clings fast and tenuous to the air.

ELIZABETH BRULÉ FARRELL

Chicken Soup

He was born in America,
his parents speaking with an accent
immigrated from another country.

He believed in waste not, want not,
and when most people threw away
a chicken carcass with no meat left

he filled a pot with water. Nothing
had to be special: celery tops with leaves,
handful of carrots, even onion skins

could bubble their way to a good stock.
He showed me so I could learn to feed myself,
not go hungry, make do with little.

He fed me books the same way: yellow
dog-eared pages from a rummage sale,
a list from the stacks at the library.

Knowledge is power, he would say,
and I learned to love memoirs and history,
how other people thought and lived

and to think about my own life through
them. Astronomy, music, politics:
companions on a journey with no end.

I did not need to understand it all, only
have a burning desire to try.

Grand Opening

Into a vacant space, the restaurant takes shape.
Small round tables, chairs, white tablecloths, paintings
of rustic villages, a fresh green awning, and they are ready.
Night after night the blonde wife and children of the Russian
sit at the tables with plates of food in front of them, staring
through the window at people who do not care to enter.
Their plates become like begging bowls extended.
Then even they stop coming and the tables stay empty.
The dogs don't like the dog food, the husband screams.
He had not known he could be so defeated,
as if by the grandmaster of chess he had seen as a child
who had found the perfect combination to crush
his opponent's mind. He remembers how he had walked
like a zombie in imitation of the loser's stunned exit
from the stage. *Me now*, he breathes, the used-up
man, sitting on the curb with his head in his hands.

JENNIFER FRANKLIN

Antigone Visits the Psychiatric Hospital

The guard confiscates the small
spiral-bound notebook I bought her

at the dollar store. The pink plastic cord
could be pulled from the pages and used

to injure herself, he explains—as if
I should have known not to bring it.

Magazines with smiling women
in swimsuits are sanctioned, as if

they will teach her how to look happy.
The music I transfer to a small silver device

makes it in but does not please her.
Vacant, she gazes past me, her thick hair

twisted in a bun. She's more beautiful
than she was at her wedding. She begs me

to get her out of the locked ward.
Says she cannot sleep one more night

in this place. The doctor asks if I
brought a word search as if finding

nouns in a field of scattered letters
could fix this. How can I tell her

I know the corners of chaos where
her mind has lured and trapped her?

How can I unpeel myself from this
vinyl loveseat and leave her

with leering nurses and patients? How
can I turn around and press the buzzer

for the guard to open the door and let me
walk out again into the strange July sun?

KATE GALE

Wound Care

Crossed to the other side of the street to avoid the wounded.
Gone to sleep to forget the wounded.

Watched the wounded on television,
Watched wounding on television.

Read fantastical stories of wounding.
Written fantastical stories of one's own wounding.

Hidden wounds up your sleeve, down your pants.
Through your body, under your socks, between your toes.

In the curve of arms and legs.
In the radius of the abdominal cavity.

Lasting wounds due to damage to underlying structures—
bone, muscle, tendon, arteries, nerves.

Cosmetic results not the primary consideration for wound repair.
Bites cause high rate of infection. Animal bites. Human bites.

We did not mean to wound others, but we did.
We wounded our friends. We wounded our lovers.

On my husband's back is a salt heart. I swim
every day in the ocean, ride behind him on the motorcycle

the salt heart where my breasts press against his shirt.
His heart has a new valve.

One long dark scar crosses his chest.
A wound of slicing deeply.

Forcing back the rib cage, taking out his heart,
replacing valve in the heart chamber with titanium.

He ticks like a clock. When I say
I have been wounded, I mean darkness.

Cherry blossoms open for fourteen days.
Petals drop. Leaves begin.

Be there for the first opening of white on pink.
Be there when the white on pink is blinding.

Be there when petals drop and green arrives.
Be there into the green and falling of leaves.

The bark sings to you. The leaves sing;
the cherry blossoms sing. Of wounding.

Of healing. Of white on pink. Of blossoms.
Feel petals blowing toward you. Feel morning come.

MELISSA HOTCHKISS

Into the Empty

If an echo happens upon itself, is recognition simultaneous?

In fractions: An echo might equal two parts acceptance, one part deep concern

It may say to itself: *Shhh . . . it's going to be OK*

As the caress of a warm salt wind can say such things

An echo may also remind itself: *There is no limit to what a body cannot feel*

And I say: A blinding beauty

MOLLY PEACOCK

Three Young Women

For Nethmie, Karthy & Madeleine

Their oval faces and full cheeks just like
the ovals in art classes teachers teach
students to draw faces with—the strike
of the chalk against the paper as fresh
as their chatter and heads bobbing *Yes*—
as world-relishing as pansies' faces
on a cold day above the mud-chilled mess
they thrive in, violet paraphrases
of what it means to grow—not yet to know,
as I do now from my irregular folds,
the energy it takes simply to spring,
eyebrows wildly arched, into being.

Let me give you something: I see you, and live.
It's not anything we can try to give, but just by looking, do.

MOLLY PEACOCK

Adult Life

On the same black rubber conveyor belt
where a hasty girl dumped her groceries
then bruised them into plastic bags, a small

thin man placed his fruit and vegetables.
Just where she'd flung her food, *his* conveyor belt
became a path into a short future.

(He was a very old man.) His oranges
and lettuces, his bell pepper and grapes
seemed to breathe themselves into being, though

they'd been severed, crated, packed, shipped and flown.
But now each seemed to have a heartbeat restored
as the conveyor bumped—his still life finished

in a minute or two (just long enough
to teach a mess of a girl staring back
at his living collage a way to live).

He'd brought a wicker basket, a thing that
would decompose, unlike her plastic bags
sulking in a dump for five centuries.

The rinds, stems, vines, leaves and peelings would decompose, too, though he'd posed them and she had
absorbed that, beginning the assemblage

of her adult life. He was her stranger,
never again seen—a deep, brief parent
who vanished as parents must, in order

to remain inside us, broken down into elements—their next life.

PATRICIA SPEARS JONES

Shack with Vines

Who lives in this motley house?
Some old woman left back of
the bottom of the county.

She's crazy. No, she's poor.
She makes her taste of something
as bitter as the broad leaves

choking the last of life from her house.

Did she go to church each Sunday?
Pull the yellow streamers during the Maypole dance?
Learn the first four chapters of Genesis
by the age of nine?

Where is her family?
Or was there not a family?
Did she nurse the folk of the county?
Is this the conjure woman, so talked about?

Or is the resident of this dying house male?
Shotgun at his bedside, ready
to blast aside the wicked.

This is his sanctuary, this little house.
Away from the highway,
far outside of town.

Far from the many temptations of the flesh,
about which he reads repeatedly in weak daylight.

Or are there orphaned children sleeping beneath blankets,
coats, whatever warmth was left behind?
They remember electricity, hot showers, macaroni and cheese.

Scavengers in the town, their T-shirts, old jeans,
and itchy, unwashed sweaters contour skinny backs.
There they are outside the local fast food drive-in

sifting through the cast-off bread and meat,
laughter tossed over the bin like an acidulent anecdote.
The shack collapsing.

PATRICIA SPEARS JONES

Painkiller

I can taste the metal
lose my desire for red meat

relax, every muscle
relax
emotion
relax
the time of day
I can give you
the time of day

What I talk about is how
love eludes me
No what I talk about is
what's wrong with me

No what I talk about is
what will happen to me

Fear
is the secret.
Always fear.

What you get from me is
the edge of a trace of shadows
and that's all you'll get

I can't give anymore
I don't want to
Everything hurts
This hurtle into living space
and that swift slide out of it.

You want secrets
I say every reckless act
results from a moment of fear.
While compassion is the simple recognition

That what is done cannot be undone,
may not be forgiven.

And a recognition that the murderer and the martyr
the adulterer and the healer can at any moment
change positions, become the other.

It simply depends on how much pain
You need to kill.

STEPHEN MASSIMILLA

About Sister

In lucid moments, she would speak
about lost nights, dungareed vagrant in the outskirts,
dreaming through girders beneath the crust of sidewalk,

waking only when the train stopped at Utica.
Arms signaling in front of her, she would rush along the rat tracks,
blue sheets of newsprint lifting in the heat.

Think back to the vacant house where she cut off
her hair: plaster scraps, blown-rose wallpaper,
folding oak ceilings, and the time

they found her even higher, in a garden on the roof
of a parking garage. Doctor Moses says
this pain leaves you the way she is left:

It never kills. Two months out of the halfway house,
she would hide inside on summer nights, lie
in the sofa's white embrace, searching its arabesque

with her nail. There were no rungs along her arm, her wrist.
But I am sure I knew more: She was the oldest,
platinum hair and a gorgeous complexion.

They said: college, marriage ahead. We would watch
her laughing, smoking, stepping into Saabs,
drawing in her silky leg. I've been searching

a landscape of cut black tunnels and moon-flooded
windows, checking the trash bars and alleyways,
asking. Along a rusty rail beneath a street-level train car

on its side like the carcass of a beast, I find tough, yellow,
cottony flowers twisting from chinks in the tracks, and part
of me urges: *Let me let her go. Let her be.*

HERMINE MEINHARD

The Sea

The child was taken while
her parents were out, carried
across the beach and never –

in the harbor
the streets empty

I wake
in the room
with the sun and wind

The children speak Spanish
We are awake now and only
need you to talk to us

* * *

I am the Eastern European
with smudged eyes

Once there was a horse

I was a bride of trees

The villagers pulled
their hair
back
from their faces

The child
was lost

A kind
of drifting took
many years

* * *

On the shore
at the hotel
sharing a plate
of shrimp, crackling
open the shells

The girls
aren't
working tonight

They braid
each other's
hair

Here is the old
metal radiator

The brothels are empty

The milk smells sweet

We eat the small
mooncakes
with butter

  We lie next to each other
hand in hand

* * *

But if I am cold?

You are not cold

* * *

In the harbor,

  a fish, twisted
    in mesh netting

 or

she, smiling,
  coming
    toward me

how lovely to be smiled at

I could sleep

her lovely voice

NANCY SHIFFRIN

Amnesty

"for what must I be forgiven?"
Lucia walked from Guatemala was shot
at the Mexican border returned again and again
until she could bribe her way North
she sits in my 6 AM class struggling
to tell her story I write her tales
on the board refuse to correct grammar
want voice hands sturdy feet
weight of eight years of hiding

soon I must teach simple present present continuous
how many stars in the flag what the stripes stand for
the students must know address social security alienation number
repeat names in the same sequence each time
demonstrate comprehension of democracy
to men who want to deport them

"for what must I be forgiven?" Lucia repeats
yet knocks on the classroom door at 5:45 eager
to speak of the mother who ripped her dress
the women whose babies she bathes
the husband who waits for her with flowers

the other students copy her story dictate theirs
all study capitals periods commas question marks
what is simple what continues
are the sweets they offer their grouchy teacher
who leads them sardonically through the Pledge

who obsesses with them on amendments and laws
who is just as terrified as they of the Test for Naturalization
who would not forgive if one were sent back

MARIA TERRONE

Your blood was no longer on the stone

under the tree when I returned to the scene today,
which didn't surprise me after last night's rain.

But still I wanted to go back to see for myself,
alone this time, no longer within the circle

of five Good Samaritans, their cell phones pulled
from pockets and bags, that calloused hand

outstretched to lift you up, the young Honduran
woman who insisted on walking us to our door,

her arm linked through yours on one side,
mine grasping the other—a kindness that washed

over us like the blessing of a downpour
after searing heat. I knelt again before that tree,

under its budding leaves, that bloodied stone
unstained now, pale gray on its patch of earth,

oddly grateful for the wound that brought strangers
to us, and me to you as you lay, later, on our bed.

When I emailed the person who'd escorted us home,
offering my thanks again—coffee or lunch

if she had the time—she didn't reply. She'd vanished
into our neighborhood of immigrants,

most ignored by longtime residents like us,
some praised, others maligned.

"Angels act, then disappear," Father Santos said
when I told our story, a smile crossing his face,

and I wondered if priests speak of angels with irony.
But I know this person in her white high tops

walks and falls to the same earth we do, this stranger
who wanted no thanks, nameless and numinous.

Not a Small Voice

ELIZABETH ALEXANDER

Amistad

After the tunnel of no return
After the roiling Atlantic, the black Atlantic, black and mucilaginous
After skin to skin in the hold and the picked handcuff locks
After the mutiny
After the fight to the death on the ship
After picked handcuff locks and the jump overboard
After the sight of no land and the zigzag course
After the Babel which settles like silt into silence
and silence and silence, and the whack
of lashes and waves on the side of the boat
After the half cup of rice, the half cup of sea water
the dry swallow and silence
After the sight of no land
After two daughters sold to pay off a father's debt
After Cinque himself a settled debt

After, white gulf between stanzas

the space at the end

the last quatrain

ELLEN BASS

Because What We Do Does Not Die

This is not his face. This is not his breath.
This is a praise song
for the mother who sat down beside me,
her coat still on,
asking, *What is it, Ellen?*
This is homage to the mother
who hissed, *The bastard. The son of a bitch,*
I'm sorry you didn't bite his tongue off.
This is not his smell or the smell
of the grass he cut.
This is my mother the next day
in her clean blouse and crimson lipstick
waiting for him in the store,
quarts of clear vodka stacked behind her.
If you ever touch Ellen again, I'll tell your wife.
This is my mother pronouncing my name,
the name she crowned me.
If you see her on the street, cross
to the other side.
The man protested.
He needed the job. *I only kissed her.*
This is how I bow down to my mother,
my dead mother who will never be dead.
I never saw him again.
This is not his voice. This is not his tongue.

HALA ALYAN

Aleppo

I talk back to the videos. Someone ate paper. Someone isn't eating anymore.

Mornings like this, I wish I never loved anyone. What is it to be a lucky city, a row of white houses strung with Christmas lights.

There is no minute.

A fortune teller told me I'd marry one of Aleppo's sons. That was seven years ago.

To spare.

Yesterday I dreamt my grandmother was a child who led me by the hand to a cave. Inside I found the wolf. I buried a dagger in his hot throat.

This is the dark world I let in, and learned

:: to stomach
:: to shoulder
                   :: to keep

I woke up with my hands wet.

They are just.

This ugly human impulse to make it mine.

Hours away.

The Syria in my grandmother is a decade too old. When she dies, she will take it with her.

This is how a lone bomb can erase a lineage: the nicknames for your mother, the ghost stories, the only song that put your child to sleep.

No one is evacuating me.

Your citadel fed to the birds. Your mosque. Someone will make an art project out of your tweets.

My daughter.

The prophet's birthday arrives without a single firework.

Surrender. Or die.

Or die.

In the city bombs peck the streets into a braille that we pretend we cannot read. A streetful of

:: girl bodies
         :: mattresses
                :: cooked hearts

Meanwhile, the wolf sleeps in his wolf palace. He drops each ghost into a waterhole and licks his perfect teeth.

We were

a free

people

We could paper all of Arkansas with your missing.

May you give us nowhere else to look. May you burn every newspaper with your name on it. Every textbook. Every memorial.

This too.

HALA ALYAN

Post-Election Morning

Gray against gray.

It's easy to make the world say what you want it to.

~

Hell hath no fury

my brother's piano fingers splayed against his laptop

like a white American

a T R U M spidering across a prayer room

that feels unimportant

~

I will [deport] myself

U.S. Census, White: A person having origins in any of the original peoples of
Europe, the Middle East, or North Africa

~

the conversations on the Q train
on campus
on a bench in midtown where one might stop to lower cheek to shoulder

~

my mom said the police were bringing tear gas so I
this is what democracy
a school where, like, like every other kid has undocumented parents
it's just, god, my daughter keepsasking
even the word pussy

~

My husband's beautiful face. We've joked that any children of ours will take my last name. There's no *P* in Arabic. I snap the photograph before midnight. In the bedroom, we move our bodies the way Allah intended. He can't come [with me]. *What's wrong,* I keep asking, *what's wrong.* He can't speak.

O sweetheart

the realization a jolt in my throat

O sweetheart you believed in America

~

My mother lost her wedding dress after Saddam
I can't throw mine away

I know you see me pulling that armful of silk out of the closet

I know you see me standing in that unlit window   America

I see you too

REGINALD DWAYNE BETTS

Prison

Prison is the sinner's bouquet, house of shredded & torn
  Dear John letters, upended grave of names, moon
  Black kiss of a pistol's flat side, time blueborn
& threaded into a curse, Lazarus of hustlers, the picayune
Spinning into beatdowns; breath of a thief stilled
  By fluorescent lights, a system of 40 blocks,
  Empty vials, a hand full of purple cranesbills,
Memories of crates suspended from stairs, tied in knots
Around street lamps, the house of unending push-ups,
  Wheelbarrels & walking 20s, the daughters
  Chasing their father's shadows, sons that upset
The wind with their secrets, the paraphrase of fractured,
  Scarred wings flying through smoke, each wild hour
  Of lockdown, hunger time & the blackened flower.

REGINALD DWAYNE BETTS

Sometimes It's Everything

Time & what else moves man to shape scrap
metal into god's tongue? Call it a bid:
slang for a stretch, a mandatory minimum that leaves
        years swollen into the thirty seconds
it took to kill, & reasons are worthless once
        cuffs close wrists, after a night's dirt turns

played-out war story for the body left owned by
        a cell's straight lines & right angles, & no one
cares for nothing, not about parole chances
        wrapped in time's chastity belt, or secrets
clock-eyed soap dice tell when they stop dead on
        snakes, or why the block is always still,

a casket of seconds, echoes, fists or nothing & chants.

JASWINDER BOLINA

Homeland

At twenty weeks in utero, the deft ovaries incorporating
inside the industrious embryo have already assembled
the six to eight million eggs they'll ever produce
in their lifetimes, of which only three or so hundred
thousand persist at puberty, of which only three
to four hundred are ever ovulated, and so half of me
made landfall in a small city in the central province
of my mother contained within the borders
of my grandmother, the three of us together there
in the village in Punjab where we didn't know English
or hunger or each other. I didn't know the other side
of my own mind, but later, the Americans tell me
you're an American if the first gulp you ever take
is of the American air above an American earth,
and so, I became an American and spoke
and swaggered as an American, and everywhere I go,
I'm greeted as an American except in America
where the Americans still see the village in my skin,
the October night my mother emigrated out
of my sweet, old gran whose sovereign womb
is another home I can't return to. Now who will
tell me God isn't a mother? Now who will say
go back where you came from?

NANCY L. COOK

About Literacy

For my birthday I received a slim volume of verse.
            When I run my thumb along the binding
                        I absorb lifetimes of effort from within:

Parchment scrolls of ancient Greeks, Hammurabi-era tablets
            made of clay, precision inks of cloistered monks,
                        and Gutenberg's democratizing type.

If how to write, how to preserve, how to duplicate
            and share weren't challenges enough, think
                        of all the hurdles built of arrogance and fear.

In my hand, I hold this gift from my friend, a preacher,
            great-great-granddaughter of slaves, a feminist
                        and skeptic: proof of just how far we've come.

My life is shared with other friends who squander time
            huddled over screens and tablets, scraps of
                        paper napkin if that's the only thing in reach.

They concentrate on language, struggle with the infinite
            varieties of words in combination; hours, days,
                        for weeks, and years, they hew and hone.

In my hand I hold the evidence, tangible and soft,
            a deceptively slim volume, binding that
                        which mortals have spent lifetimes

trying to perfect.

ROSALIND BRENNER

Women's Music

In Jaffna, I met a woman in a black burqa,
baby strapped across her breast.
I caught the sack of oranges
as it fell from her arms.
Her smile was in her gaze, her voice.

In the bustling café, another woman
sat alone at a communal table.
Her deep brown eyes showed through a slit.
She slipped a dripping spoon of rice
under her niqab to find her mouth.

I've read there are lands
where women are jailed or stoned
if they attempt to heed the lyrics
of their dreams.

Old hippie, tourist, Western feminist,
the songs I sing
are not hymns of faith.
Not psalms of praise
under the protective eyes
of brother, father, husband.
I sing in opposition
to the way men rule.

I have spun in drum circles.
I have shouted, I have cried,
fought for identity,
caught in the injustice of men's gazes,

the way they stared and gestured.
Unwelcome catcalls when I was young.
The way they do not see me now.

Jaffna woman, do you feel like singing
so loud you entertain the neighbors?
Do you need permission to stand
before your mirror, unrestrained and naked,
slip on a pair of bright red dancing shoes,
shuffle around the kitchen for the fun of it?
Can you hear music in the beat of silence
draped in winter black?

We are every mother, you and I.
Let's sing sweet lullabies
to our babies, suckle them,
wish for our daughters
the power to compose
their own melody, their own refrain.

TINA CANE

Rage and Ibuprofen

I know little   about matters   of practical application

it was being a waitress   that taught me   how to get along

that people want their food   and want it now   like everyone

my mind has regions

one for meat   one for bread

one for caravans   and tender age   one for rage

and ibuprofen

plus a whole zone for listening

past the migraines   to the dog whistles in the air   faint toll

of cowards ringing across time   history has to start somewhere

so, why not here?   I ask

my class to write

a letter to Mr. Baldwin   because *time catches up*

with kingdoms and crushes   also because I miss him

one girl writes:

Dear James,

The most courageous thing
a person can be is a black woman.

Damn, son   says the boy   at the desk behind her

and we all sit in silence   until the bell rings

PAOLA CORSO

Arrival

1.

January 1, 1892. A teenager from Ireland
and her two younger brothers
    skip two steps at a time

      up the main staircase to Ellis Island.

A chorus of foghorns
peals of church bells
    steam whistles & cheers

      as the first immigrant passes through.

"What is your name, my girl?"
"Annie Moore, sir."
    Registry book signed

      handed a ten-dollar gold piece

chaplain's blessing
wishes for a happy new year
    escorted to the waiting room

      into the arms of her parents.

2.

May 20, 1905. A Polish woman
with three little children
    climbs the steps

       from the pier to Ellis Island.

Baggage room, registry room
more steps to Public Health
    as she takes

       a six-second physical—how

quickly she climbs the stairs
how high she lifts her legs
how tightly she grips the railing

how labored her breath.

Next a test for intelligence. The question: "Would you
wash the stairs from the top down or the bottom up?"
    The woman's curt reply:

    "I do not come to America to wash stairs."

3.

The Immigration Act of 1924. A stone mason from Sicily
climbs the steps from the pier to Ellis Island.
　　　If he were given the same physical

and asked the same question

he would think of hundreds of steps
he built from the sea to his hill town,
　　　an Italian's pyramid

to the heavens.

Then he could answer: "I come to America
with mallet and chisel. No broom."
　　　But a doctor measures his head and body parts.

　　　Too short. Too dark and hairy. Ears too big.

A commission concludes that certain kinds of behavior
are inherent in the Italian race.
　　　Crimes of violence, robbery, blackmail

are peculiar to the people of Southern Italy.

A "natural born criminal" climbs down
the steps from Ellis Island to the pier.
　　　Savage, the report says, and a rapist.

　　　Rejected.

KWAME DAWES

Land Ho

I cannot speak the languages
spoken in that vessel,
cannot read the beads
promising salvation.

I know this only,
that when the green of land
appeared like light
after the horror of this crossing,

we straightened our backs
and faced the simplicity
of new days with flame.
I know I have the blood of survivors

coursing through my veins;
I know the lament of our loss
must warm us again and again
down in the belly of the whale,

here in the belly of the whale
where we are still searching for homes.
We sing laments so old, so true,
then straighten our backs again.

KWAME DAWES

Talk

For August Wilson

No one quarrels here, no one has learned
the yell of discontent—instead, here in Summer
we learn to grow silent, build a stone
of resolve, learn to nod, learn to close
in the flame of shame and anger
in our hearts, learn to petrify it so,
and the more we quiet our ire,
the heavier the stone; this alchemy
of concrete in the vein, the sludge
of affront, until even that will calcify
and the heart, at last, will stop,
unassailable, unmovable, adamant.

Find me a man who will stand
on a blasted hill and shout,
find me a woman who will break
into shouts, who will let loose
a river of lament, find the howl
of the spirit, teach us the tongues
of the angry so that our blood,
my pulse—our hearts flow
with the warm healing of anger.

You, August, have carried in your belly
every song of affront your characters
have spoken, and maybe you waited
too long to howl against the night,

but each evening on some wooden
stage, these men and women
learn to sing songs lost for centuries,
learn the healing of talk, the calming
of quarrel, the music of contention,
and in this cacophonic chorus,
we find the ritual of living.

TOI DERRICOTTE

On the Turning Up of Black
Unidentified Female Corpses

Mowing his three acres with a tractor,
a man notices something ahead—a mannequin—
he thinks someone threw it from a car. Closer
he sees it is the body of a black woman.

The medics come and turn her with pitchforks.
Her gaze shoots past him to nothing. Nothing
is explained. How many black women
have been turned up to stare at us blankly,

in weedy fields, off highways,
pushed out in plastic bags,
shot, knifed, unclothed partially, raped,
their wounds sealed with a powdery crust.

Last week on TV, a gruesome face, eyes bloated shut.
No one will say, "She looks like she's sleeping," ropes
of blue-black slashes at the mouth. Does anybody
know this woman? Will anyone come forth? Silence

like a backwave rushes into that field
where, just the week before, four other black girls
had been found. The gritty image hangs in the air
just a few seconds, but it strikes me,

a black woman, there is a question being asked
about my life. How can I
protect myself? Even if I lock my doors,
walk only in the light, someone wants me dead.

Am I wrong to think
if five white women had been stripped,
broken, the sirens would wail until
someone was named?

Is it any wonder I walk over these bodies
pretending they are not mine, that I do not know
the killer, that I am just like any woman—
if not wanted, at least tolerated.

Part of me wants to disappear, to pull
the earth on top of me. Then there is this part
that digs me up with this pen
and turns my sad black face to the light.

TOI DERRICOTTE

Why I don't write about George Floyd

Because there is too much to say
Because I have nothing to say
Because I don't know what to say
Because everything has been said
Because it hurts too much to say
What can I say what can I say
Something is stuck in my throat
Something is stuck like an apple
Something is stuck like a knife
Something is stuffed like a foot
Something is stuffed like a body

RITA DOVE

The Breathing, the Endless News

Every god is lonely, an exile
composed of parts: elk horn,
cloven hoof. Receptacle

for wishes, each god is empty
without us, penitent,
raking our yards into windblown piles ....

Children know this, they are
the trailings of gods. Their eyes
hold nothing at birth then fill slowly

with the myth of ourselves. Not so the dolls,
out for the count, each toe pouting from
the slumped-over toddler clothes:

no blossoming there. So we
give our children dolls, and
they know just what to do—

line them up and shoot them.
With every execution
doll and god grow stronger.

CORNELIUS EADY

Diabolic

> *"Their colour is a diabolic die."*
> —Phillis Wheatley

What they say they are
And what they actually do
Is what Phillis overhears.
It's like she isn't there.
It's like she's a ghost, at arm's length, hearing
The living curse out the dead—
Which, she's been led to believe
No decent person does in a church.

How they say they love her
And how they look at her
Is what Phillis observes;
Like she's the hole in the pocket
After the money rolls out.

God loves everybody—even the sinner,
(they say)
Even a mangy hound can rely
On a scrap of meat, scraped off the plate
(they say).

What they testify
And what they whisper in earshot
Is as dark as her skin, whistled from opposite sides
Of a mouth.

Is she the bible's fine print?

CORNELIUS EADY

Tubman's Rock

I held visions; I too was chosen
And tossed against my say-so.
Who knew I'd be carried
All those years, or my kiss could form a scar
On her forehead, or that I'd sing to her at
Unwelcome times?

Our meeting was brief;
A rough hand wished her dead
And aimed.
I startled and fell. Here I nest, spent
In a field,
Special among
My kind. Her hard lesson, her God-flint.

ROSS GAY

A Small Needful Fact

Is that Eric Garner worked
for some time for the Parks and Rec.
Horticultural Department, which means,
perhaps, that with his very large hands,
perhaps, in all likelihood,
he put gently into the earth
some plants which, most likely,
some of them, in all likelihood,
continue to grow, continue
to do what such plants do, like house
and feed small and necessary creatures,
like being pleasant to touch and smell,
like converting sunlight
into food, like making it easier
for us to breathe.

ROSS GAY

Pulled Over in Short Hills, NJ, 8:00 A.M.

It's the shivering. When rage grows
hot as an army of red ants and forces
the mind to quiet the body, the quakes
emerge, sometimes just the knees,
but, at worst, through the hips, chest, neck
until, like a virus, slipping inside the lungs
and pulse, every ounce of strength tapped
to squeeze words from my taut lips,
his eyes scanning my car's insides, my eyes,
my license, and as I answer the questions
3, 4, 5 times, my jaw tight as a vice,
his hand massaging the gun butt, I
imagine things I don't want to
and inside beg this to end
before the shiver catches my
hands, and he sees,
and something happens.

MARIA MAZZIOTTI GILLAN

Jayden de Leon, Age 7,
The Herald News, Wednesday, March 2, 2016

Jayden de Leon, age 7, lived on Rosa Parks Boulevard
with his mother and his sisters.
Jayden was shot through a window following a commotion
outside his house, a three-story multi-family across the street
from a liquor store and a car repair shop.

Everyone in the apartment, Jayden's grandmother
and great-grandmother, his sisters, his cousin
was hysterical, but Jayden asked for the phone,
called 911, said "I've been shot" and gave his address.

The police and ambulance arrived within minutes.
Jayden remained calm throughout.
His mother said, "I know the streets are dangerous,
too many drugs, but I can't afford to move."

For many, the street where Jayden lives
offers cheap, stopgap housing.

"It is a place to leave," neighbors said.

Empty lots line both sides of their house.
Patches of grass with empty bottles
of Remy Martin and Budweiser.
Cars rumble by blasting loud music.

Two blocks to the north is School 10.
One block north is Church of God of Prophecy.
"If you want to live here, you've got to be a survivor,"
a 15-year-old neighbor, Frederick David said,
"it's straight surviving."

JUAN FELIPE HERRERA

Half-Mexican

Odd to be a half-Mexican, let me put it this way
I am Mexican + Mexican, then there's the question of the half
To say Mexican without the half, well it means another thing
One could say only Mexican
Then think of pyramids—obsidian flaw, flame etchings, goddesses with
Flayed visages claw feet & skulls as belts—these are not Mexican
They are existences, that is to say
Slavery, sinew, hearts shredded sacrifices for the continuum
Quarks & galaxies, the cosmic milk that flows into trees
Then darkness
What is the other—yes
It is Mexican too, yet it is formless, it is speckled with particles
European pieces? To say colony or power is incorrect
Better to think of Kant in his tiny room
Shuffling in his black socks seeking out the notion of time
Or Einstein re-working the erroneous equation
Concerning the way light bends—all this has to do with
The half, the half-thing when you are a half-being

Time

Light

How they stalk you & how you beseech them
All this becomes your life-long project, that is
You are Mexican. One half Mexican the other half
Mexican, then the half against itself.

DANIELA GIOSEFFI

Don't Speak the Language of the Enemy[†]

reads the poster at the end of a grey alleyway of childhood
where the raggedy guineas of Newark
whisper quietly in their dialects on concrete steps
far from blue skies, olive groves or hyacinths.

Bent in a shadow toward the last
shafts of sunlight above tenement roofs,
Grandpa Galileo sadly sips homemade wine
hums moaning with his broken mandolin.

Children play hide-and-seek
in dusty evening streets as red sauce simmers,
hour after hour, on coal stoves,
garlic, oil, crushed tomatoes blended
with precious pinches of salt and *basilico*—
a pot that must last a week of suppers.

The fathers' hands with blackened fingernails are worn
rough with iron wrought, bricks laid, ditches dug, glass etched.
Wilted women in black cotton dresses wait in twilight,
calling their listless children to scrubbed kitchens.
In cold water flats with tin tables, stale bread is ladled with sauce,
then baked to revive edibility. Clothes soak in kitchen laundry-tubs,
washboards afloat. Strains of radio opera are interrupted by war bulletins.

The poster pasted on the fence at the end of the block
streaked with setting sun and rain reads:
"DON'T SPEAK the LANGUAGE of the ENEMY!"

But the raggedy guineas can speak no other,
and so they murmur in their rooms in the secret dark frightened
of the camps where people like them were imprisoned
in the new land of golden opportunity. They whisper of Mussolini's
stupidity—stifling the mother tongue, wounding the fathers' pride,
urging their children to speak English by daylight,
telling each other, "We are Americans. God bless America!"

[†] It's a little-remembered fact that there were internment camps for Italian immigrants in the United States during World War II, similar to those in which Japanese immigrants were incarcerated. 600,000 Italian immigrants were detained in camps or displaced, as were 120,000 Japanese immigrants.

RACHEL HADAS

Shouldering

The dream bird father sitting on my shoulder
is singing in my ear: *Now that you're older*
than I was when I left the rocky road,
it is your turn to shoulder the load,
answer questions students need to ask.
You are an elder now. You wear the mask
of wisdom. So you tell them

                    Tell them what?
The song breaks off. In somebody's back seat,
a baby. Whose? More babies on the border.
Terror, desperation, rage. Disorder
of crowded house, tap leaking, family,
students leaning in to question me:
Where should we go now? Tell us what to do.
The road's uphill, and that is all I know,
borrowing, burrowing, stirring the dark stew,
blended broth of night visions and day,
instructions garbled, watchmen standing tall
and menacing at gates along a wall.
Gaps in the rampart: raw red border zone.
Children wake and cry along the line.
The students' questions pound relentlessly.
Dream father, bird of omen, oh tell me—
the lost, the hungry, the abandoned—who
will take care of them? The grownups knew
the answers to these questions. And now
we are grown up, whose job is it to know?
The reassuring elders, where are they?
The dream bird looks at me and hops away.

Always uphill   the steep road   poetry
Scattered syllables still in my ear
when I sit up and the red world is here.

BRENDA HILLMAN

Crypto-animist Introvert Activism
a haibun

Every week for about a decade some of us at school have been standing at lunch
hour to protest drones, racism, state killing, the death of species & so on. We
stand under a live oak while people walk by on their way to lunch. We hold up
the signs. It's an absurd situation & it changes nothing.

Sometimes the good doctor Ali brings a boom box with Bob Marley & we
dance ineptly on the pavement. The changes fall together. Positive & negative
fall together as Bob Marley sustains us near the tree. César Vallejo dances as
a flea on the back of a squirrel. Blake & Baraka dance as lithophilic microbes
inside the rock. We have no proof that they don't. The science moths dance
in the live oak & go about their work of being powdery. The protest is absurd
but i admire these forms of absurdity. When the revolution comes, the polite
white mothers in the Moraga Safeway will still be shopping for sugary cereals
& barbeque sauce. When the time comes, some will rise & some will dance &
some will lay our bodies down.

SCOTT HIGHTOWER

A Spontaneous Attack, 2018

Victoria Marion
B. Sept. 6, 1988, Ruse, Bulgaria
Murdered: Oct. 6, 2018 Ruse, Bulgaria

Three investigative journalists
have been killed in the EU
in the past year. In October,

fifty-three-year-old Caruana Galizia
was killed by a car bomb in Malta.
Reporting on allegations of corruption
across the political sphere.

Galizia clearly stated: "There are
crooks everywhere you look now;
the situation is desperate," and,
within thirty minutes, she was gone.

Ján Kuciak and Martina Kusnirova, his fiancée
(in a tarot deck, they would have been
"The Lovers"), were murdered together—
shot by contract killing—in Slovakia
in February. Kuciak, 27,

reported on politicians (some
connected to Smer, the ruling party)

and businessmen involved
in tax evasion and fraud
in connection to luxury real estate.

And now, Viktoria Marinova,
a thirty-year-old, appealing,
photogenic television journalist
(who had just launched *Detector*,
a new talk show with a focus
on investigative journalism)

is brutally raped, bludgeoned,
and killed in one of the parks
on the Bulgarian bank of the Danube

after airing allegations of
fraud involving EU funds.

—

Ministers and prosecutors busily
purport, "There is no apparent
link to her work. It was
a 'spontaneous' attack."

She is survived by her parents,
two sons, and ex-husband.

*

"The murder of a journalist—
who makes revelations about those
who choose to disrespect
and break the law—is a crime,
not only against the victim,
but also against society as a whole."

The fascists, destroyers of democracy,
secretly holding the lie, are unbeatable
in the field . . . . They want all to believe
they have blown up the last enemy ring.

But one of the sequestered canisters,
rather than full of a legal pesticide . . .
is full of a lethal toxic gas;

and an investigator has
noticed that the repair putty
surrounding a window in one
of the railway barns is not dry.

Daphne Caruana Galizia (B. Aug 26, 1964, Sliema, Malta – Assassinated by car bomb: Oct. 16, 2017, Bidnija, Malta)

Ján Kuciak (B. May 17, 1990 – Shot: Feb. 21, 2018, Veľká Mača, Slovakia)

Martina Kusnirova (B. Apr. 3, 1990, Gregorove, Sovakia – Shot: Feb. 21, 2018, Veľká Mača, Slovakia)

JANE HIRSHFIELD

Spell to Be Said Against Hatred

Until each breath refuses *they*; *those, them.*
Until the *Dramatis Personae* of the book's first page says, "Each one is you."
Until hope bows to its hopelessness only as one self bows to another.
Until cruelty bends to its work and sees suddenly: *I.*
Until anger and insult know themselves burnable legs of a useless table.
Until the unsurprised unbidden knees find themselves bending.
Until fear bows to its object as a bird's shadow bows to its bird.
Until the sound the mouse makes inside the mouth of the cat.
Until the inaudible acids bathing the coral.
Until what feels no one's weighing is no longer weightless.
Until what feels no one's earning is no longer taken.
Until grief, pity, confusion, laughter, longing know themselves mirrors.
Until by *we* we mean I, them, you, the muskrat, the tiger, the hunger.
Until by *I* we mean as a dog barks, sounding and vanishing and sounding and
     vanishing completely.
Until by *until* we mean I, we, you, them, the muskrat, the tiger, the hunger, the
     lonely barking of the dog before it is answered.

MAJOR JACKSON

In the Eighties We Did the Wop

If you end your crusades for the great race,
then I will end my reenactments of flying,
and if you lean down to smell a painted trillium,
then I will cast a closer eye on those amber waves,
and if you stop killing black children,
then I will turn my drums to the sea and away from
your wounded mountains. Who mothered your love of death?
Here is a heart-shaped stone to rub when you feel fear rising;
give me anything, an empty can of Pabst, a plastic souvenir, a t-shirt from Daytona.
Here is a first edition: *The Complete Poems of Lucille Clifton*.
Give me an ancient grove and a conversation by a creek, charms
to salve my griefs, something that says you are human,
and I will give you the laughter in my brain and the tranquil eyes of my uncles.
Show me your grin in the middle of winter.
In the eighties we did the wop; you, too, have your dances.
It is like stealing light from a flash in the sky. I promise:
no one is blaming you. No one is trying to replace you.
It's just that you are carrying a tainted clock calling it *European History*,
standing in khakis, eyes frightened like a mess of beetles.

HONORÉE FANNONE JEFFERS

An Issue of Mercy #1

Mercy, girl.
What the mother might have said, pointing

at the sun rising, what makes life possible.
Then, dripped the bowl of water,

reverent, into oblivious earth.
Was this prayer for her?

Respect for the dead or disappeared?
An act to please a *genius child*?

Her daughter would speak
of water, bowl, sun—

light arriving,
light gone—

sometime after the nice white lady
paid and named her for the slave ship.

Mercy: what the child called Phillis
would claim after that sea journey.

Journey.
Let's call it that.

Let's lie to each other.
Naked travail among filth and rats.

What got Phillis over that sea?
What kept a stolen daughter?

Perhaps it was *mercy*,
Dear Reader.

Mercy,
Dear Brethren.

Water, bowl, sun—
a mothering, God's milky sound.

Morning shards, and a mother wondered
if her daughter forgot her real name,

refused to envision the rest:
baby teeth missing

and somebody wrapping her treasure
(barely) in a dirty carpet.

'Twas mercy.
You know the story—

how we've lied to each other.

YUSEF KOMUNYAKAA

The African Burial Ground

They came as Congo, Guinea, & Angola,
   feet tuned to rhythms of a thumb piano.
      They came to work fields of barley & flax, ,

livestock, stone & slab, brick & mortar,
   to make wooden barrels, some going
      from slave to servant & half-freeman.

They built tongue & groove — wedged
into their place in New Amsterdam.
      Decades of seasons changed the city

from Dutch to York, & dream-footed
   hard work rattled their bones.
      They danced Ashanti. They lived

& died. Shrouded in cloth, in cedar
   & pine coffins, Trinity Church
      owned them in six & a half acres

of sloping soil. Before speculators
   arrived grass & weeds overtook
      what was most easily forgotten,

& tannery shops drained there.
   Did descendants & newcomers
      shoulder rock & heave loose gravel

into the landfill before building crews
came, their guitars & harmonicas
chasing away ghosts at lunch break?

Soon, footsteps of lower Manhattan
strutted overhead, back & forth
between old denials & new arrivals,

going from major to minor pieties,
always on the go. The click of heels
the tap of a drum awaking the dead.

YUSEF KOMUNYAKAA

Dead Reckoning III

They work fingers to bone & borrow
smudged paper, then make promises
to family, unmerciful gods, the unborn.
Some eat a favorite meal three times
in a row. Others partake only a pinch
of soil before boarding half-broken boats
& rubber rafts—half of the young women
big with life inside them, flesh & blood
for daydreams of the Arabian nights,
as makeshift charts & constellations
work their way through war & rumors
of war. The smugglers count their loot.
Hard winds rattle gongs over sea salt
till the rusty engines die, & cries alert
mermaid sirens as pirated schooners
adrift under a mute sky rock to & fro,
& the fight goes out of the few alive.
Their loved ones & friends, lost folk
songs, mountains & valleys, all left
behind. Searchlights spot the dead
hugging the living, & draglines raise
only those who were braver than us.
The lucky ones stumble out of stupor,
tried by raging water beneath black
skies, listening to the albatross talk.

DEVI S. LASKAR

in praise of the B in Bengali
For TZA

Because B is for the Bengali we no longer understand and the borders that
neither contain nor define us.
Because B is for Bangladesh, a nation founded on the idea Bengali is a Beautiful
language worth saving. 1971.
Because B is for our silk saris Billowing, the enormity of our responsibilities
piling up around us.
Because B is for the Broad strokes we make with our pens as we practice our
cursive English, for the Broad strokes we make with our arms as we swim on our
Backs in chlorinated American pools.

Because B is for Bangladesh, a nation founded on the idea Bengali is a Beautiful
language worth saving. 1971.
Because B is for Beauty in the flames of change, Burning Brightly through the
nights.
Because B is for the Broad strokes we make with our pens as we practice our
cursive English, for the Broad strokes we make with our arms as we swim on our
Backs in chlorinated American pools.
Because B is for Bengali literature and Tagore who won a Nobel Prize in 1913.

Because B is for Beauty in the flames of change, Burning Brightly through the
nights.
B is for the manmade, hand-drawn Boundaries that were never real.
Because B is for Bengali literature and Tagore who won a Nobel Prize in 1913.
B is for the Bengali that is slanted between us, I understand what you say and
you nod when I Butterfly my tongue in a way to pronounce something your
mother used to say.

B is for the manmade, hand-drawn Boundaries that were never real.
B Because I am sorry for the way I Behaved.

B is for the Bengali that is slanted between us, I understand what you say and you nod when I Butterfly my tongue in a way to pronounce something your mother used to say.

There are no words of greeting and thanks in Bengali. We borrow from Sanskrit, we borrow from Hindi. Namaste, we say. Dhanyabaad, we say. And the ignorant fools with license to drive and buy assault weapons mistake our shared word for thanks as the capital of a rogue nation. Every day is actually four days after 9-11, when a Sikh man was killed in Arizona for the turban he wore on his head.

B Because I am sorry for the way I Behaved.

Because B is for an incomprehensible Muslim Ban.

There are no words of greeting and thanks in Bengali. We borrow from Sanskrit, we borrow from Hindi. Namaste, we say. Dhanyabaad, we say. And the ignorant fools with license to drive and buy assault weapons mistake our shared word for thanks as the capital of a rogue nation. Every day is actually four days after 9-11, when a Sikh man was killed in Arizona for the turban he wore on his head.

B is for Being indistinguishable in the eyes of all those who perpetuate the white gaze.

Because B is for an incomprehensible Muslim Ban.

B is for the substance of what I have spoken, lost in the Bay of Bengal every morning and evening as thousands cross over from East to West in escape, in search of something Better.

B is for Being indistinguishable in the eyes of all those who perpetuate the white gaze.

B is for the teacher telling us to Begin again, write in a language that is not your own, assume nothing But the language of our colonizers.

B is for the substance of what I have spoken, lost in the Bay of Bengal every morning and evening as thousands cross over from East to West in escape, in search of something Better.

In Bengali language is vasa the s pronounced sh as in shh as in the first of the shooting star or the last of a whirling dervish.

B is for the teacher telling us to Begin again, write in a language that is not your own, assume nothing But the language of our colonizers. In Bengali véshé is somewhere Between sailing and flooding, swimming and drowning, somewhere between riding the last wave to shore and having that wave crest blue over you forever.

In Bengali language is vasa the s pronounced sh as in shh as in the first of the shooting star or the last of a whirling dervish.

Because B is for our silk saris Billowing, the enormity of our responsibilities piling up around us.

In Bengali véshé is somewhere Between sailing and flooding, swimming and drowning, somewhere between riding the last wave to shore and having that wave crest blue over you forever.

Because B is for the Bengali that we no longer understand and the borders that neither contain nor define us.

ADA LIMÓN

A New National Anthem

The truth is, I've never cared for the National
Anthem. If you think about it, it's not a good
song. Too high for most of us with "the rocket's
red glare" and then there are the bombs.
(Always, always there is war and bombs.)
Once, I sang it at homecoming and threw
even the tenacious high school band off key.
But the song didn't mean anything, just a call
to the field, something to get through before
the pummeling of youth. And what of the stanzas
we never sing, the third that mentions "no refuge
could save the hireling and slave"? Perhaps
the truth is that every song of this country
has an unsung third stanza, something brutal
snaking underneath us as we blindly sing
the high notes with a beer sloshing in the stands
hoping our team wins. Don't get me wrong, I do
like the flag, how it undulates in the wind
like water, elemental, and best when it's humbled,
brought to its knees, clung to by someone who
has lost everything, when it's not a weapon,
when it flickers, when it folds up so perfectly
you can keep it until it's needed, until you can
love it again, until the song in your mouth feels
like sustenance, a song where the notes are sung
by even the ageless woods, the shortgrass plains,
the Red River Gorge, the fistful of land left
unpoisoned, that song that's our birthright,
that's sung in silence when it's too hard to go on,

that sounds like someone's rough fingers weaving
into another's, that sounds like a match being lit
in an endless cave, the song that says my bones
are your bones, and your bones are my bones,
and isn't that enough?

DEVI S. LASKAR

Taking the Poem from the Poet

What if I tell you they didn't evacuate
the high school after he brought in
the clock? What if he and clock waited
in the principal's office
until the police came? You look at me
as though I pulled the fire alarm,
yelled into a crowded theatre. You
think I can erase the weapon out
of the hands of that young man in
Kevlar pointing his assault rifle at me?
Would your pain lessen? Would you
sleep tomorrow? What if I expunge
the hoodie? Outlaw convenience
stores? Institute curfew for all adult males
after 8 P.M.? Did you know that kid
loved horses, ate Skittles, went to
aviation camp? What if
I rub out midnight of the blue, blue
world? Take the jaywalk from the boy
trying to catch a city
bus? Which blue should it be? First or
second? The last thing you hear on the radio
before mashing
another button? What if there were no loosies
to smoke, steal, hawk? What if Sandy used her signal?
I say her name, I canonize the thought all
black lives matter. What if I raise my
voice? What if I don't stop speaking?
What if I stop talking back?
Then will you miss me?

MARIA LISELLA

A Stitch in . . .

It required a stitch or two and so
I tacked it the way my mother taught me.
A seamstress in a different age,
she'd tailor and sew and design
in a union shop, a safe place.
This shirt was sewn at a different
time, halfway around the world.
The two tabs stuck out
of my friend's cheap striped shirt.
Made in Bangladesh read the label
where women who know nothing
about raised fists of labor united or
the IWW, or the AFL-CIO, sweat
for 14 hours a day and 35 cents an hour
turning out shirts just like this one.
The labels read: H&M, Calvin Klein,
Ann Taylor, Zara, Target.
Yet when factories go up in flames
or crumble into tangles of steel,
concrete blocks, mortar,
with detritus fizzling with the
stench of human flesh and bone
for weeks maybe months in New Delhi,
Bangladesh, Ahmedabad, label-owners
deny those very same women had
anything to do with earning them
the $2.4 trillion dollars in profits
they report each year on garments
with tabs untacked, seams unraveling.

MARIA LISELLA

They Don't Remember When We Were . . .

. . . the immigrants, the sharecroppers,
the unskilled laborers standing on corners
waiting for work, maybe it was the Hell's Gate Bridge
or the dangerous bowels of the subways.

Sharing low-lit tenements with men piled high
swapping pillows, sheets and beds as they returned
from the morning shift, the evening shift,

the stench of those men-filled quarters.
No women to dress for, to clean for,
to shave for, a society of men clammy

in winters, sultry in summers, saving
meager wages split with padroni
and landlords, before sending bits and pieces

home to bring wives and children
here to this foreign place, trying
to remember why they left home,

was it that bad? Yes it was. Wives don't tell
the men in their letters of the famine,
the deaths, a silk thread of hope spanning

the Atlantic, to feel whole again
not so alone, to be human instead
of imitating animals in the daily routine:

Wake, work, sleep, nothing in between
no rises or falls or celebrations or
clean towels or bread on the table

set for four, six or set at all.
Eating while standing becomes a skill
on the corners waiting for the work

if the policeman doesn't move them
to another corner, stepping into strangers'
cars, a dangerous deal for a day's work.

Now the men speak with accents from
Mexico, Guyana, India, but they are not
so different from our grandfathers and uncles

shifting from one foot to the other to keep warm
expecting a day's pay by nightfall, but who can tell?
They have no choice.

My mother recalls the stories of her father, brothers.
She cannot understand the nieces, nephews
who don't see their ancestors' faces before them.

STEPHEN MASSIMILLA (After Neruda)

The Workers of Macchu Picchu
After Neruda

Like corn, the mortals were husked in the bottomless
granary of forgotten deeds, miserable events,
from one o'clock to seven, to eight,
and not one but many deaths came to each:
every day a small death—dust, worm, lamp
snuffed in the slums of mud—a small thick-winged death
entered each laborer like a short lance,
and these men were driven by bread and by the knife,
by the rancher, son of the seaports, dark captain of the plow,
like rodents of overrun streets:
all weakened waiting for their death, their brief daily death;
and the fateful ageing and fading of each day was
a black cup from which, all trembling, they drank.

STEPHEN MASSIMILLA (After Montale)

The Hitlerian Spring[†]
After Montale

"Nor she who turns to see the sun ..."
—Dante (attributed), in a sonnet to Giovanni Quirini

A thick fog of maddened mayflies
swirls around dirty lamps and over the parapets.
Underfoot, they form a shroud that crackles
like sugar. Spring slowly frees
the nocturnal frost
from caverns, ghosted gardens
extending from Maiano to these shores.

Up the street, an infernal messenger just flew by,
flanked by curdling cries of *Heil!* Concealed
like the Wagnerian orchestra pit
at one of his mad midnight rallies, a mystical gulf
lit up and flagged with mangled crosses just embraced him,
gulped him down.

This evening all the shop windows
are shuttered—
though even these are armed
with cannons and little military toys.
A man has bolted his gate. He is a friendly butcher
who would garland the muzzles
of slaughtered goats with grapes:
Easter rite for those still unaware that the blood
has utterly changed: Shattered wings
and larvae on the banks; the water goes on chewing
at the shoreline.

Everything we had was all for nothing, then? The Roman candles
at the San Giovanni festival slowly whitening out
the horizon, and our pledges and lingering good-byes—
binding as a baptism in the mournful presence
of the horde (though a budding comet rayed the air, distilling
on the ice and the rivers of your New World shores
the angels of Tobias, the seven, yes, the seed
of the future)
                        . . . and the heliotrope unfolding
from your palms—all scorched, sucked dry
by this pollen that hisses like fire
and bites with the teeth of a blizzard . . .
No one is blameless anymore.

                                    This ulcerated
spring is festive even if it freezes
all this death in death! Look again:
up there, Clizia, lies your destiny, you
who keep love so unaltered in its alteration
until the blind sun you carry inside you
can bedazzle the Other and explode
in Him, for all—or for you,
at least, at least.

Maybe the sirens, the pealing bells
that saluted monsters
at their Sabbath, are already dissolving
in the celestial sound that—unleashed—descends and conquers
with the breath of a dawn that tomorrow may rise again

for all—bleached, of course, but please without swarms
of gnawing terror, in the parched river bottoms of the south . . .

† Loosely after Montale's *"La primavera hitleriana."* The verb "frees" in the first stanza suggests
hope for the imminent liberation of Italy from fascism. The cellars are those of the partisans.
Maiano lies six miles outside Florence. Honored at an annual festival, San Giovanni (to whom
the baptistry of Florence Cathedral is dedicated) is the patron saint of the city. Hitler was
the "infernal messenger," Mussolini the warlock leader of the other "monsters." The tale of
Tobias and the guardian angel from the Catholic Old Testament involves travel, healing, and
the transformation of seven demonic deaths into seven hopes. Clizia (Clytie) is the sunflower-
woman in Greek mythology, Montale's Beatrice, modeled on Irma Brandeis, a glamorous Jewish
American Dante scholar. Clizia is leaving for America to escape persecution and death. There is
hope that American troops will land in southern Italy.

NAOMI SHIHAB NYE

Two Countries

Skin remembers how long the years grow
when skin is not touched, a gray tunnel
of singleness, feather lost from the tail
of a bird, swirling onto a step,
swept away by someone who never saw
it was a feather. Skin ate, walked,
slept by itself, knew how to raise a
see-you-later hand. But skin felt
it was never seen, never known as
a land on the map, nose like a city,
hip like a city, gleaming dome of the mosque
and the hundred corridors of cinnamon and rope.
Skin had hope, that's what skin does.
Heals over the scarred place, makes a road.
Love means you breathe in two countries.
And skin remembers—silk, spiny grass,
deep in the pocket that is skin's secret own.
Even now, when skin is not alone,
it remembers being alone and thanks something larger
that there are travelers, that people go places
larger than themselves.

ELISE PASCHEN

Kitihawa

"Monday May 10th 1790 Stopt at Point Sables anchord with the cannots &
begun to hull Corn & bake Bread & arranged everything for next Morning..."
—Hugh Heward's Journal from Detroit to Illinois: 1790

My relatives guide fur traders between swamp
and bog, down age-old trails, under pine trees
and black oaks, navigating the tributaries,
the sweeps and turns. My husband and I

followed the river to its mouth, this spot
where the sun and the moon climb above
the rim of lake. I feed the traders hot
loaves from our Bakery, milk crocks from our Dairy.

Silent as fog rising from the marsh, I observe.
The traders barter canoes for our whitewood dugouts.
My husband broods at the prow of the long table,
candles sputtering, reflected between two mirrors.

Clearing the wooden plates, I question the way they shake hands.
I see blazing greed, our earth parched, my descendants gone.

PAISLEY REKDAL

有 識: Have Knowledge

From the immigration questionnaire given to Chinese
entering or re-entering the U.S. during the Chinese Exclusion Act

Have you ridden in a streetcar?
Can you describe the taste of bread?
Where are the joss houses located in the city?
Do Jackson Street and Dupont run
in a circle or a line, what is the fruit
your mother ate before she bore you,
how many letters a year
do you receive from your father?
Of which material is your ancestral hall
now built? How many water buffalo
does your uncle own?
Do you love him? Do you hate her?
What kind of bird sang
at your parents' wedding? What are the birth dates
for each of your cousins: did your brother die
from starvation, work, or murder?
Do you know the price of tea here?
Have you ever touched a stranger's face
as he slept? Did it snow the year
you first wintered in our desert?
How much weight is
a bucket and a hammer? Which store
is opposite your grandmother's?
Did you sleep with that man
for money? Did you sleep with that man
for love? Name the color and number
of all your mother's dresses. Now
your village's rivers.

What diseases of the heart
do you carry? What country do you see
when you think of your children?
Does your sister ever write?
In which direction does her front door face?
How many steps did you take
when you finally left her?
How far did you walk
before you looked back?

SONIA SANCHEZ

This Is Not a Small Voice

This is not a small voice
you hear   this is a large
voice coming out of these cities.
This is the voice of LaTanya.
Kadesha. Shaniqua. This
is the voice of Antoine.
Darryl. Shaquille.
Running over waters
navigating the hallways
of our schools spilling out
on the corner of our cities and
no epitaphs spill out of their river mouths.

This is not a small love
you hear   this is a large
love, a passion for kissing learning
on its face.
This is the love that crowns the feet with hands
that nourishes, conceives, feels the water sails
mends the children,
folds them inside our history where they
toast more than the flesh
where they suck the bones of the alphabet
and spit out closed vowels.
This is a love colored with iron and lace.
This is a love initialed Black Genius.

This is not a small voice
you hear.

SOLMAZ SHARIF

He, Too

Returning to the US, he asks
my occupation. Teacher.

What do you teach?
Poetry.

I hate poetry, the officer says,
I only like writing
where you can make an argument.

Anything he asks, I must answer.
This he likes, too.

I don't tell him
he will be in a poem
where the argument will be
anti-American.

I place him here, puffy,
pink, ringed in plexi, pleased
with his own wit
and spittle. Saving the argument

I am let in
I am let in until

PETER SCHMITT

Conversation in Camden County

Across the street from Whitman's house
the women stand both day and night,
moving their hands through the air: eyes
squinting at the slit-like windows
high above them, recessed and dark,
behind which their men (husbands, sons,
lovers and brothers and fathers)
presumably can see them too,
each having found from his small cell
down some stale, dim corridor of
Camden County Correctional,
his own woman, small and recessed
herself, on the street or sidewalk
below, but his, and speaking now
in the signed speech she had to learn
and teach to him—their only means
between rare official visits.

The women stand, one diapering
her child on the hood of a Dodge,
relaying the household events,
the small details of their stalled lives,
the pinched budget, the child's new cough,
each speaking in the strange language
of the unhearing, to those mute
in their own way but hanging, there,
high up, on each hand-spun word, flesh
of each face pressed to the meshed glass.

And they keep on standing, the streetlights
shuddering on, on past midnight
sometimes, these women, their tired backs
to the gray clapboard two-story,
whose occupant they may never
have heard of, who would have himself
stood with them, speaking with his hands
if no other way—patient too,
for those who will return, those men
who will not. All of them, women
and the old homesteader, would stay,
until their wrists ached, lifting each
unguarded word toward these men
they cannot see, whom they only
can trust to be there, still, waiting.

HILARY SIDERIS

Questions for the Wanda Coleman Test

*"You were magnificent, Pop. You never won the title belt, but at heart
you were the truest gentleman champion I've ever known."*

Define *brain fever, candy
striper.* Explain why there's no bed

at Charity Children's Hospital
for the deliriously ill, eleven-year-old

Wanda. Define *lynch mob.* Explicate
the look on the guard's face

when her father, Light Heavyweight
Champion Archie Moore's

sparring partner, says *My child is dying.
Be decent, be a man.* Contrast

how his shoulders in worn wool
make Security & Wanda feel.

MERVYN TAYLOR

Gum

In American war movies, chewing gum was
a sign of staying calm while bullets whizzed
overhead, a symbol of the kindness of GI's,
as they passed out sticks of it to wide-eyed kids.

In Minnesota, while a policeman kneeled on
George Floyd's neck, one of the officers kept
chewing, as Floyd called to his deceased mother
that he was dying. And recently, a black woman,

just out the shower, stood in her living room
shivering, the broken door letting in light,
policemen in a ring around her as she screamed,
Wrong house, you got the wrong house!

And though the sergeant used his jacket to cover
her shoulders, she'll never forget their faces,
especially the one who never stopped smiling
and chewing gum, who never once looked away.

MERVYN TAYLOR

That One

How they picked one back then
was by fondling the balls
the penis the calves by running
their hands along the flanks
as you would horses by looking
into the mouths the other orifices
pretending it wasn't exciting
not the thrill of a Saturday
afternoon not a good break
from the boring breeze blowing
through the weeping willows
not a chance to see in the flesh
the cargo that came in chains
from the other side of the world
passed through a door into hell
the sea as if in a kettle boiling
the green land disappearing
in a gulp gone the last hut like a
dream upon waking to the touch
of a strange hand the scent
of a perfume upon a skin so
translucent the veins snaking
in grey rivers through the swamps
of moss that hung in beards
off the magnolias as in whispers

the wives advise this one
this one for the bulbous knots
on his arms for the pulsing drum
of the heart visible just beneath
the sternum for the vacancy
in the rooms of his eyes as
they search for the wife the child

not quite seven, for the ridge
of a spine that will answer the lash
with its own grimace its own inimitable
dance in returning to the tree
where its buried navel string
climbs like a vine you can see now
if you go there, these many years after.

MERVYN TAYLOR

How the Gun Is Like the Taser

I watch the parents of the boy
cry, who wish they could go
back in time, who wish to

rewind, so the car he was
driving wouldn't start, so his
wisdom tooth would choose

that day to break through his
gum, and pain to the point he
would go and lie down. And

the woman who shot him, that
the dark pit of a trench would
open up across her yard

like a seam of coal, so she'd
have to go back in, unstrap the
belt, ponder the weight of

the gun vs. that of the yellow
taser, reverse the order in
which they hang on her torso,

so the universe would start
spinning backwards, releasing
black bodies from their graves.

MARIA TERRONE

Afghan Shadows

At the fundraiser, the famous TV reporter
told us the woman's story:
forbidden to record a female face,
she interviewed her in shadow,
the woman's hands

doing most of the talking.
Newly widowed, the woman hoped to remain
nameless, but her unique wedding ring
gave her away. So they locked her
indoors, nailing wooden boards

across the windows, blocking even her shadow.
After cocktails and dinner,
the woman's teenage daughter stood before us.
All clinking and murmur stopped
in the glittering hall as she grasped

for the right words in a strange language
to pull herself up, as if from a pit.
My murdered father and *our prison*
were the first to prick me, leaving their small
but unmistakable entry wounds.

Her mother lives now behind the walls
of an Afghan women's refuge
where her body moving in sunlight
casts a shadow again, and her mind
slowly leaves the shadows behind.

LAURA TOHE

Little Sister

For Frank LaMere

In 1984 the body of twenty-one year old Michelle LaMere from Winnebago, Nebraska was found in north Omaha where she had been run over by a car.

I was the youngest of nine children. The morning they found me, the mulberries had already given away their young fruit. And summer was a smooth, slender, dark woman dancing to the center of the drum. My grandfathers' voices still rise above the rolling hills along the Niobrara where my people dance.

But my voice was invisible against the onslaught. Their words lie. They create divisions, arrange my life in numbers, add and subtract me, and put me into neat boxes for storage.

My life unraveled early alone in a large city where I followed shadows and chased the jagged promise of empty bottles. There, I thought
I heard my father's voice softly calling "Baby, baby, you're my baby"
when my mother first unwrapped me, a newborn present,
a young heartbeat to strengthen the drum.

In the blossoming light the earth goes on gathering the dripping fruit of mulberries in her outstretched arms along the Niobrara. In the season of gathering mulberries, I danced the fury of buffalo and dreamed the slender, dark woman, and my brother singing, singing in the voice of praise:

> Little sister, little sister,
> > tasted her life again
> > in the spiraling dance of thunder beings,
> > and buffalo
> > and was borne away into the

thunderclouds
and the rain that
fell and fell
afterwards.

NATASHA TRETHEWAY

Letter Home

New Orleans, November 1910

Four weeks have passed since I left, and still
I must write to you of no work. I've worn down
the soles and walked through the tightness
of my new shoes calling upon the merchants,
their offices bustling. All the while I kept thinking
my plain English and good writing would secure
for me some modest position. Though I dress each day
in my best, hands covered with the lace gloves
you crocheted—no one needs a *girl*. How flat
the word sounds, and heavy. My purse thins.
I spend foolishly to make an appearance of quiet
industry, to mask the desperation that tightens
my throat. I sit watching—

though I pretend not to notice—the dark maids
ambling by with their white charges. Do I deceive
anyone? Were they to see my hands, brown
as your dear face, they'd know I'm not quite
what I pretend to be. I walk these streets
a white woman, or so I think, until I catch the eyes
of some stranger upon me, and I must lower mine,
a negress again. There are enough things here
to remind me who I am. Mules lumbering through
the crowded streets send me into reverie, their footfall
the sound of a pointer and chalk hitting the blackboard
at school, only louder. Then there are women, clicking
their tongues in conversation, carrying their loads
on their heads. Their husky voices, the wash pots
and irons of the laundresses call to me.

I thought not to do the work I once did, back bending
and domestic; my schooling a gift—even those half days
at picking time, listening to Miss J—. How
I'd come to know words, the recitations I practiced
to sound like her, lilting, my sentences curling up
or trailing off at the ends. I read my books until
I nearly broke their spines, and in the cotton field,
I repeated whole sections I'd learned by heart,
spelling each word in my head to make a picture
I could see, as well as a weight I could feel
in my mouth. So now, even as I write this
and think of you at home, *Goodbye*

is the waving map of your palm, is
a stone on my tongue.

GEORGE WALLACE

He Remembers the Sun, the Only Light He Sees

sometimes the gods sing, sometimes the gods laugh, sometimes a
man takes a drink as night gnaws deep into his bones, because his
frustration is dark as a sea of blood, because he cries out for the light
of some inheritance that only he sees

he who possesses an entire world in the palm of his hands, he who
owns the gold in his teeth and the frost in his mouth, he who grinds
corn with his molars until the corn is stolen from him

no he cannot trust anyone, only the sun which goes up and down like
a gypsy violin, the sun which he used to love; he was a child, how the
sun would shake and dive like a river swallow racing through summer
light, from daybreak to sunset, and he raced along with the sun, he
was a child, free!

they are singing in the tavern, a shepherd song, they are singing on a
hillside, a soldier's song, bravo bravo bravo the revolution, bravo bravo
bravo the people!

take up your glass, little man, fill up your time, drink deep, two hands
deep, you too shall make the gods sing and laugh, you too shall make
companions and martyrs out of men, and strike back at the usurpers'
hearts of clay, hands that shake, how they shake, and night is terrible,
even now a god casts a long shadow across the table, because the gods
appear when the heart of a man has turned to clay

and of course the injustice, there is always the injustice, anyone can
smell it, any man who is a man can taste it and it cannot be tolerated
or spit out, injustice over tabletops, injustice across valleys, injustice
over the hearts of men and the astonished bodies of women

and revolution is a seamstress stitching men together, and the sound of an entire village weeping, as village upon village stands motionless and accusative in the hallway while you drink in the shadows which are not your own

and the dogs of war hungry for flesh, and the fields barren and the armies lurking, and motorcades with flags flying, and motorcycles and generals wearing sunglasses

take to the mountains! take up your weapons! simple men, solid men! come on man, you!

he puts his hands to his face, he can feel the loose gravel of his father's grave, he can smell the feral soil which his father's father has returned to, enriched, become; this man who puts his tongue to the roof of his mouth and his mouth is dry and tastes like blood; this man whose heart is cold; a revolution is about to start, nations shake when he lights his cigar, mountains burn when he empties his glass.

darkness at the window, and he remembers the light of the sun, the only light he sees.

GEORGE WALLACE

For This My Heart the Revolution

I bury the passion, i scrape the flesh, i set free the words that come out of my mouth, i go into the world, I speak in future tenses, like anger and surprise and men in *huaraches*, my shoulders cry, my cheeks sprout feathers, i am the monster my children and grandchildren learned to love and fear, to conjure up like wind, to cultivate their days like fields of rice, i listen in the dark, i let their dying be, i am the cry of lightning, fermentation in the eagle's nest, in the kitchen of the world beans fall from my plate, spoons scrape a tin cup, and the children are at it again, and the sun rises, the sea falls

Sometimes the sky is very still, and i am an icon in a church that has known no name and the women sing verses to me, the children dance in a circle, this is a song which i have never heard, i say grace with the women, i pray for their children, i explore their bodies like bullet holes, pray! pray for the river, pray for the fruit which is my flesh, i have known no other body but this one, i have loved and been loved, gather around my bed and do not try to touch me, my sweat is my testimony, i am a bunkhouse in an open sky, my eyes penetrate deep into the earth like miners

Blood and semen is mine and i am a man, i pour myself out of my bed and into the pit of men i go, naturally, i have prepared myself a long time for this, 3500 hundred years is a teardrop in my eye, before there was heaven there was us, before us, a river

I prepare myself for this
For love, for death—for this
My heart the revolution

MARJORY WENTWORTH

One River, One Boat

In memory of Walter Scott and Muhiyyidin d'Baha

"I know there's something better down the road."
—Elizabeth Alexander

Because our history is a knot
we try to unravel, while others
try to tighten it, we tire easily
and fray the cords that bind us.

The cord is a slow-moving river,
spiraling across the land
in a succession of S's,
splintering near the sea.

Picture us all, crowded onto a boat
at the last bend in the river;
watch children stepping off the school bus,
parents late for work, grandparents

fishing for favorite memories,
teachers tapping their desks
with red pens, firemen suiting up
to save us, nurses making rounds,

baristas grinding coffee beans,
dockworkers unloading apartment-size
containers of computers and toys
from factories across the sea.

Every morning a different veteran
stands at the base of the bridge
holding a cardboard sign
with misspelled words and an empty cup.

In fields at daybreak, rows of migrant
farm workers standing on ladders break open
iced peach blossoms; their breath rising
and resting above the frozen fields like clouds.

A jonboat drifts down the river.
Inside, a small boy lies on his back;
hand laced behind his head, he watches
stars fade from the sky and dreams.

Consider the prophet John, calling us
from the edge of the wilderness to name
the harm that has been done, to make it
plain, and enter the river and rise.

It is not about asking for forgiveness.
It is not about bowing our heads in shame,
because it all begins and ends here:
while workers unearth trenches

at Gadsden's Wharf, where 100,000
Africans were imprisoned within brick walls
awaiting auction, death, or worse.
Where the dead were thrown into the water,

and the river clogged with corpses
has kept centuries of silence.
It is time to gather at the edge of the sea
and toss wreaths into this watery grave.

And it is time to praise the judge
who cleared George Stinney's name,
seventy years after the fact,
we honor him; we pray.

Here, where the Confederate flag
flew beside the Statehouse, haunted
by our past, conflicted about the future;
at the heart of it, we are at war with ourselves

huddled together on this boat
handed down to us—stuck
at the last bend of a wide river
splintering near the sea.

YVONNE

Norman Rockwell and Me[†]

Not white, my first school day dress had been
Dark plaid cotton, Mother's genuflection
To season and weather—September's green
Humid soup. And my shoes, a brown
Sturdy leather with laces, had to last 'til June.
Still, Rockwell's girl could have been my twin.
White schoolhouse doors, my steppingstone
With Mother, not government men.

A navy blue wool jumper, on second thought,
Was my first school day outfit. Mother bought
A white blouse, too, then marched me where nuns taught.
"It's January. She just turned six and can count."
Mother never blinked; so that was that.
The portrait girl walked with much more debate.
From my white school days, she was ten years late.
In grownup twists and turns both of us caught.

From winter to spring one child's face
And name yet blooms in that first grade class.
Theresa Z. A bump in her nose,
Brown hair cut short, to keep out of her eyes,
Barrette on the side—how sharp my eye still is!
Some days I might wait for her fancy rowhouse
Door to open and we'd stroll together in grace
Talking ribbons and dolls and Christmas.

Could I visit and play? Her mom asked mine.
OK. But did Mother propose in kind?
Our crisscross curtains equally refined?
In hindsight, probably not. But why decline
Sliding boards, monkey bars, and swings—all behind
A high watchdog fence? The drift in the wind
I can only guess, though Mother could defend
My friend. Did the projects offend? Even then?

So, how did I meet Cookie? The project playground?
Where else? Her mom, "straight out the Great Depression,"
Mother guessed. "Stringy hair, crooked teeth, sunken
And raw-bone." She let Cookie and her brother come
Over for TV because they didn't have one
Yet. Willie the Worm, Krazy Kat, Kukla, Fran
And Ollie, Farmer Alfalfa. Any cartoon
Wilder than Hickok, Lone Ranger, Kit Carson? None.

The projects. Deep in the city my every day
Was filled with shady trees between school and play
Because Mother never broke her rule: "Never stay
Two nights under a *colored only* sign." Did free
Clouds shower, free sun spin—equally
On our three yellow rooms in the projects? Maybe.
How else—without hoopla, without one dot of stray
Spit—I survived sixteen years . . . then Rockwell's hooray?

[†] *The Problem We All Live With* by Norman Rockwell, an illustration in *Look* magazine, January 14, 1964, commemorates the day Ruby Bridges integrated an elementary school in New Orleans by court order. Rockwell's *New Kids in the Neighborhood* is an illustration for an article on integration in the suburbs for *Look*, May 16, 1967.

KEVIN YOUNG

Nightstick [A Mural for Michael Brown]

There are gods
   of fertility,
corn, childbirth,

& police
   brutality—this last
is offered praise

& sacrifice
   near weekly
& still cannot

be sated—many-limbed,
   thin-skinned,
its colors are blue

& black, a cross-
   hatch of bruise
& bulletholes

punched out
   like my son's
three-hole notebooks—

pages torn
   like lungs, excised
or autopsied, splayed

open on a cold table
    or left in the street
for hours to stew.

A finger
    is a gun—
a wallet

is a gun, skin
    a shiny pistol,
a demon, a barrel

already ready—
    hands up
don't shoot—

arms
    not to bear but bare. Don't
dare take

a left
    into the wrong
skin. Death

is not dark
    but a red siren
who will not blow

breath into your open
   mouth, arrested
like a heart. Because

I can see
   I believe in you, god
of police brutality—

of corn liquor
   & late fertility, of birth
pain & blood

like the sun setting,
   dispersing its giant
crowd of light.

i'd tell you

KIM ADDONIZIO

High Desert, New Mexico

Temple of the rattlesnake's religion.
Deluge and heat-surge. Crèche of the atom's
rupture. Night blackens like a violin
and bright flour falls from the kitchens of heaven.
This is where the seams begin to loosen,
where you can walk for miles in any direction—
rabbit, lizard, raven, insect drone—
and almost forget the shame of being human.
Smoke tree. Sage. Not everything is broken.
Horses appear at this remote cabin
to stand outside and wait for you to come
with a single apple. Abandon
your despair, you who enter here forsaken.
The wind is saying something. Listen.

ELIZABETH ALEXANDER

Blues

I am lazy, the laziest
girl in the world. I sleep during
the day when I want to, 'til
my face is creased and swollen,
'til my lips are dry and hot.
I eat as I please: cookies and milk
after lunch, butter and sour cream
on my baked potato, foods that
slothful people eat, that turn
yellow and opaque beneath the skin.
Sometimes come dinnertime Sunday
I am still in my nightgown, the one
with the lace trim listing
because I have not mended it. Many days
I do not exercise, only
consider it, then rub my curdy
belly and lie down. Even
my poems are lazy. I use
syllabics instead of iambs,
prefer slant to the gong of full rhyme,
write briefly while others go
for pages. And yesterday,
for example, I did not work at all!
I got in my car and I drove
to factory outlet stores, purchased
stockings and panties and socks
with my father's money.

To think, in childhood I missed only
one day of school per year. I went
to ballet class four days a week
at four forty-five and on
Saturdays, beginning always
with plié, ending with curtsy.
To think, I knew only industry,
the industry of my race
and of immigrants, the radio
tuned always to the station
that said, Line up your summer
job months in advance. Work hard
and do not shame your family,
who worked hard to give you what you have.
There is no sin but sloth. Burn
to a wick and keep moving.

I avoided sleep for years,
up at night replaying
evening news stories about
nearby jailbreaks, fat people
who ate fried chicken and woke up
dead. In sleep I am looking
for poems in the shape of open
V's of birds flying in formation,
or open arms saying, I forgive you, all.

ELLEN BASS

Ode to Invisibility

O loveliness. O lucky beauty.
I wanted it and I couldn't bear it.
When I was a girl, before self-serve gas,
as the attendant leaned over my windshield,
I didn't know where to look.
I could feel his damp rag rubbing the glass
between us. Or walking from the subway,
even in my work boots and woolen babushka,
all those slouched men plastered to the brick walls
around the South End of Boston—
I could feel them quicken, their mouths
opening like baby birds. I was too beautiful
and never beautiful enough.
Ironing my frizzy hair on the kitchen table.
All the dark and bright creams to sculpt my cheekbones,
musk dotted on my hot pulses,
and that pink angora bikini that itched like desire
as I laid myself down under the gold of a sky we didn't yet fear.
Hello, my pretty. Your ankles were elegant,
your breasts such splendor
men were blinded by their solar flare.
These days, I'm more like my dog,
who doesn't peruse himself in the mirror,
doesn't notice the gray at his temples, though I think
it makes him look a little like Cary Grant in *Charade*.
I can trot along the shallow surf of Delray Beach
in my mother-in-law's oversize swimsuit,
metallic bronze and stretched-out so it bulges like ginger root.

On one side, that raucous ocean surging and plunging,
on the other, the bathers gleaming with lotions and oils.
I can be a friend to them all, even the magnificent young,
their bodies fluid as the curl of a wave.
I can wander up to any gilded boy, touch
his gaudy bicep, lean in confidentially. I'm invisible
as a star at noon, a grain of clear sand.
It's a grand time of life: not so close to the end
that I can't walk for miles along the pulpy shore,
and not so far away that I can't bear
the splendid ugliness of this disguise.

JASWINDER BOLINA

Waiting My Turn

I remember telling Hillary how I'd rather be
the 23rd turbaned astronaut than the first

setting out to be the 239th man on the moon

in my second-hand pressure suit, in my hand-me-down
helmet, oversized and swiftly lifted over the coast

of Arizona, all the interns yawning at their stations

in the humdrum easy of Ground Control,
my khaki rocket routinely returning

to rest on its pad, wiser, more worldly

for its exertion, for sure, but when it says,
Boy, I seen everything now, boys,

to the shiny new rockets, they're gassing up,

readying for Neptune, thinking, *The* moon??
Everybody's been to the goddamn moon,

while I am 239,000 miles away,

stepping out of my blanched canister
onto the lethal grit of the goddamn

moon, mumbling, *At last.*

It's my *fucking turn at last.*

GRACE CAVALIERI

Just This

The water to the left turning
then to the right past barbed fences
leaning through trees once again alive
up then down the valley you like
what you see spring summer
it doesn't matter to walk by the water
is to see white seasons turning green to blue
swarms of flying sparks with wings in the
closing darkness then morning comes
past your sight verging so we want to close
our eyes then to open to find some meaning
find purpose for movement and we slow down
then we find there is no meaning but motion.
Just this. Again, and again. Just this.

TINA CANE

Treatise on My Mouth

Turns out I am   *chargé d'affaires*

of my own mouth   of my real speech

though I sometimes think   I am just being

emotionally concise   that my powers

of constraint   are not about   protecting

my own interests   but instead   entail purity

or poetry
                    but we'll let your mouth

be the judge of that   I am sure there's a test   or an app

I should probably   ask my kids   for whom my policy

is never to be
                    alarmist

rather to appear   as a fact witness   to our lives

so that I can tell them   what they were like   when they

were little
                    to be a regular channel

of love   is my intention   for I am here   to avoid

long-term conflict   while propagating   a narrative of truth

by means   of my one and only   mouth   worthy of attention

I am ready to answer your questions

RUTH DANON

Knowledge Is Power

All day we have been talking,
One way or another, about heat.
We wanted, at first, a two-faced
Woodstove, one that would warm
One room and another at the same
Time. Then we thought of two
Woodstoves, easier to install, less
Damage to the structure of the rooms.
Those who know me know
That I fear nothing more than I fear
Cold. We decided on two stoves
That could be installed at different
Times, that would serve different
Needs. We all have needs but they
Are not always the same needs.
My need is to avoid cold. My need
Is not to be afraid of what I fear.

                  Later we talked
About fear, how some are afraid
To walk down dark streets at night,
Or afraid to step outside of the
House now that the whole world
Is sick. My fear seems small, just
The cold frightens me. They say
That the thing we fear is what will
Kill us. In the hospital where I
Spent too much time I begged
For warm blankets. Sometimes
They had them. Sometimes not.
I will always, no matter what,
turn up the heat.

JENNIFER FRANKLIN

Biopsy Pantoum

I am waiting for biopsy results again—
in the mirrored room where time stalls.
Knowing women are always at the mercy of men,
even after I get the results, it will feel like my fault.

In the mirrored room where time stalls,
I stare at the same insipid face.
Even after I get the results, it will feel like my fault.
I walk the treadmill, regretting what I can't erase.

I stare at the same insipid face.
The longer I carry my body, the harder it is to tend.
I walk the treadmill, regretting what I can't erase
Until I die, this worry will never end.

The longer I carry my body, the harder it is to tend.
Knowing women are always at the mercy of men,
until I die, this worry will never end.
I am waiting for biopsy results again.

TOI DERRICOTTE

I give in to an old desire

I lost so much
of the world's beauty, as if I were watching

every shining gift
on its branch with one eye. Because

I was hungry. Because I was waiting

to eat, a self

crawling about the
world in search

of small things. I remember a small thing, my mother's hat,

a tea-
hat or cocktail

hat that sat on top of her
perfect face—petals, perhaps

peonies flaming out, like
the pink feathers of some exotic

bird. Her mother
had been a cook in the South. She grew up

in the home of
wealthy white people. Hesitant

toward her own
beauty, unable

to protect mine, there were things
she never talked about. She said silence

was a balm. It sat
on top of her head, something of exaltation

& wonder exploding
from the inside like

a woman in orgasm. One artificial flower

I have desired
to write about for years.

TOI DERRICOTTE

The Weakness

That time my grandmother dragged me
through the perfume aisles at Saks, she held me up
by my arm, hissing, "Stand up,"
through clenched teeth, her eyes
bright as a dog's
cornered in the light.
She said it over and over,
as if she were Jesus,
and I were dead. She had been
solid as a tree,
a fur around her neck, a
light-skinned matron whose car was parked, who walked on swirling
marble and passed through
brass openings—in 1945.
There was not even a black
elevator operator at Saks.
The saleswoman had brought velvet
leggings to lace me in, and cooed,
as if in the service of all grandmothers.
My grandmother had smiled, but not
hungrily, not like my mother
who hated them, but wanted to please,
and they had smiled back, as if
they were wearing wooden collars.
When my legs gave out, my grandmother
dragged me up and held me like God
holds saints by the
roots of the hair. I begged her

to believe I couldn't help it. Stumbling,
her face white
with sweat, she pushed me through the crowd, rushing
away from those eyes
that saw through
her clothes, under
her skin, all the way down
to the transparent
genes confessing.

JANE HIRSHFIELD

The Bird Net

I once decided to pretend to be angry.

Then I was.

As a bird is caught in its birdness before it is caught in the bird net.

The bird might be counted, tagged, released.
The bird might be eaten.

It took hours for the shaking to leave my body.

Body of air, body of branch, what earth's yellows & nectars were made for.

TESS GALLAGHER

Sully

*"It hurts me to think of you
under the ground."*
—Jaime Sabines

My view of you is always aerial
like time to a child who surrounds
everything with promise. I'm above
you like a ceiling fan and you—laid out
as my father described you—on the only flat
surface in the house, the kitchen table—like
a banquet to which everyone is invited
but to which no one can sit
down. For the record, my father told us

your death as if it were the heaviest
grief of his young life. He'd been away working
in the Iowa coal mines, then come home on a whim
to the Oklahoma farm where you lived,
taking care of the youngest children. Sully,
a half-sister, that demotion—your mother dead, your father's
bride sending child after child
toward your protecting hands. "She did everything

for us," my father told us, so I saw she was their
de facto mother. She wouldn't have known
her half-relation status as anything but
bounty—her future already lodged

in her—that she would have no children.
So I hover above you, Sully.
one of my long undeclared loves, because
my father declared you in his quiet account

of having walked toward that house surrounded
by cars, the question weighing on him
as he approached: what happened? Through
the door then (and now his children
with him in his telling), your black hair
as in a García Lorca play, rayed out
on the white pillow. He tells us
of your coward lover, who took you

to the quack doctor with this result. How it
quenched my child heart to suffer your
death like that. Did you guess your story
would pass to anyone as words in air,
you who were bound in the amber of your
will to help everyone around you, not
extending yourself more truly than that? If
a poem could kiss dead eyes awake, you'd

come back to me here in the house my father
built, thousands of miles from where you
were buried. And because time is both fire
and star, you'd open yourself like a music box
given to a child for nothing but delight. You'd

tell me how it is in the round of time,
to live outside it all in the beauty and sadness
your name carries when I remember

it in my father's voice each time he brought you
back to us. Sully. His soft saying of it—so you
are alive and dead at once—you whom
the world tried to squander, but failed

in just this dimension: that if I were to say
your name aloud in this solitary room
where my father's hammer, its exact singing
steel to steel, came down
on every board, some air of you
might wake from the dead and speak.

JENNY MOLBERG

Epistle from the Hospital for Harassment
To B.L.

As in a house of mourning / cover the mirrors / Save yourself from yourself / Open the windows / Feed your history to the night / Do not wrestle
/ against your story / let it keep happening / then kill it—/ the poet who
invited you for coffee / a manila folder of poems / meticulously typed /
and tucked beneath your arm / all those beats and breaks / silenced / as
he thrust his hand on your hip, saying Sweetheart, try your hair in a bun /
and What about glasses / If you wore glasses men wouldn't notice you so
much / Or your colleague who poked / a bruise on your thigh / guessing at
its origins / Or the man who made the bruise / Honey, you're not as stupid
as you look—/ Cast it out / until the night is so full of the feathers of your
thoughts / it grows the giant wings of a crow / takes off—/ Now lie before
the curtained mirrors / Forget what you look like / For better is a wander-
ing eye / than the two you clench shut / waiting for him to finish

JENNY MOLBERG

May the Stars Guide You Safely Home

After I call the cops to ask for a protective order
I read about the girlfriend of a serial killer. What she knew,

what she didn't. How it seems we're always punished
for asking questions. America is watching a show

about a man who is fascinating. His eyes ice
behind the fog of his glasses.

Such a nice guy. Such a quiet guy. The flooded house.
I don't care about him. I want to say their names:

Ann Bryan. Katherine Ann Hall.
Hardee Schmidt. Joyce Williams.

Lillian Robinson. Marilyn Nevil.
Johnnie Mae Williams. Donna Bennett Johnston.

When I call the cops
I hold my arm like a seatbelt. When I call the cops

a woman answers. Hand over chest like an elementary
school lie: the pledge, the flag, the wrong math.

The girlfriend rode in the car and didn't know
about the woman in his trunk. Not two people there,

but three. When I call the cops the officer speaks like an aunt,
Honey, don't you know this only makes it worse?

The law provokes, a split tongue made of amendments.
As a child I used to dream

of walking down my city street, past the newspaper
stand, to our corner house with its porthole window,

the garage that spilled open like a mouth. I'd ring
the doorbell and another mother would answer, her children

like impressions of me. I thought I lived there.
The system is turning me to sand.

Honey, if I were you I'd sit tight, get a gun. The killer's girlfriend
killed a man once. The author of the book about the killer

says she liked the feeling of being desired.
He might as well say she was asking for it.

A biker in a Sons of Silence jacket broke a pool cue
over the girlfriend's back so she fought and then she was fighting

not a man but an idea, not one thing but many,
and then the man was dead. She carried

his photo in her wallet for years. We're watching the show
of America because we want to win.

To win means kill and not be killed.
This helps the system. The court believes the bad actor.

Before I call the cops I call a domestic abuse advocacy center.
They say *conflict of interest*. They say *he got there first*.

I try to say it's all backwards.
I try to say please listen to me.

The night of the hearing I awake thinking
I am the girlfriend, the silence of the trunk

an ocean. It takes hours to rise, to gather myself,
part by part, pulling the truth from the dark.

This is my face. This is my name.
Someone loves me.

My voice is animal in the courtroom microphone.
Behind the judge, the sideways prison of the flag.

MILLER OBERMAN

"If this was a different kind of story i'd tell you about the sea"
—Marwa Helal

1.

I look at it every day and still can't tell you much. Today a figure out on the
jetty is shadowboxing, hitting wind, running down the boulders that break it,
crouching in crevices, springing up to kick spray. It's beautiful, but not only. I'm
too tired for similes this morning. What, I want to ask, did air ever do but hold
you, what did waves ever do but be tireless come and come, come and come?

2.

I learned this as a child. Dirt and sand, air and waves treated me the same as
everyone, my body not expected to be like anything, free from meaning aside
from being. "What are you," the green broad leaves asked no one ever. The sky
boundless blue or domed gray and spitting ice hit every kid the same, those
whose skins and names and genders lay neat as feathers, vanes perfectly directed
outward from the inner quill, and those of us whose plumes seemed dis-arranged.

3.

I dislike to speak of it, I may dislike speaking of it more even than I dislike it to
have happened that on this island where I was born those boys quietly climbed
[   ] behind my back and [   ] my swing at its apex. The air held us all the
same though I was not the same, that was their point when [   ] I not seeing
gone flung [   ] in air, layers of gases, water vapor I was not [   ] harder than
any other in the elastic scattering of light and gravity while [   ] watched
and turned away in [   ] let us practice punishing and being punished. I have
thought since then how sensible that the word "shame" begins with the same
sound that ends the word "punish." That mute shuffle, the edgeless shadow, the
convulsing shake of a diaphragm with all its wind knocked out.

4.

I want my children, your children, even those boys' children uncrushingly to fit within their structures, but how good a father can I be when last summer at the beach I saw two boys chucking a football, shirtless and seeming joygold and free as the waves and I felt pangs at their perceived ease, knowing nothing of their troubles or fears. If only my blood beat even as the sea, faithfully lapping in valves, foaming safe in chambers. Now I am a man, I remind myself. And those are not the boys, any of the boys who had me choking on the lightness of air. My father had ease like that, at least in photos. After he died I tried to write a poem that imagined all my selves as separate bodies, each standing on the shoulders of the previous one. It was mainly a description of shoes. A good place to try this would be in salt water, but I don't see time that way anymore, at least I don't want to. I want something less ponderous, less vertical, like how the sea cannot fall down, and I would forget their names and stand in the surf like a gull.

PAISLEY REKDAL

Hall of Sea Nettles

Darkness indicates
there's beauty to be praised
in these displays of bell-
    shaped blooms
    that float through rooms
of indigo lit

      so as to stage the fragile
colors: violet whips and pale
mouth tentacles: trails
    of blush peach lace
    that flume the upturned,
tumbled cups—

    A guide proclaims
their heads—part
water, part collagen—
    lack excess bits
    like bones or brains (*Stupid
as the senate*, one onlooker

    quips), whose charm lies in
how subtly they move.
Proved by this gap-mouthed crowd
    of various ages pressed
    together in the gloom to catch
each sinuous

            unloosening, a sash
of pink nerve net or vellum
ribbon tossed by sudden
            jetted sprays.
            Every jelly
shivers, streams.

    A parent snaps
as one boy's finger
steams at the glass.
Mothers emphasize the sting.

Ambitions

Liverpool

I. In '62, my young mother flew from known melodies, from clouds rolling up and down the Mersey with the tides.

II. Where would I be otherwise? Each curved person a lattice of contingency. Weak sunlight filters through.

III. She was born in a curved iron and glass shed, Lime Street Station platform eight London Midlands, with a hissing exhale and a rocking momentum.

IV. Corridors of red sandstone, arched brick, concrete bearded with soot and moss. Four pairs of rails rusted pink. The city's muscles contract.

V. Towers topped with empty nests. Where are the birds?

VI. My return ticket bought by her departure. My diplomas. My pay stub. My upwardly-mobile American refusal to pick up after men.

VII. Brakes whine softly until the country opens and I pick up speed.

VIII. Far away, joint-sore, she is throwing off a duvet, opening blinds, creaking downstairs to her son's kitchen, listening to news of brutal collusions.

IX. Daisies, buttercups, yarrow—flowers that cannot be suppressed—and sheep-cropped hills beyond.

X. Clouds are heavy, sorrowful. They resist breakage but wind has its own ideas. Look at the azure vents it opens, with a tearing cry.

Ambitions

Bath

I.   So that my brother William Herschel may concentrate on becoming a famous astronomer.

II. Grind and polish mirrors, perform calculations, and wash lace cuffs. Read Alice B. Toklas while a mute swan drifts through reflections on the Avon.

III. Practice the stillness of the gilt head of Sulis, sleeping for centuries in a sewer.

IV. Pray to her for wisdom or at least the heat of the sun.

V.   Consider prayer. A question etched on a lead tablet. Water wells up in reply. Whose water? What will happen if I drink?

VI. When my daughter the physics star was born, Hale-Bopp glowed in the sky. A maternity nurse wrapped me in blankets. We witnessed the brilliant tail.

VII. Pack cheese baps for the coach to Heathrow. Roll children's blouses neatly for cases. Be an ordinary woman. The sacred spring's water tastes of boiled eggs.

VIII. Be an ordinary comet-hunter. Consider how to gather available light, to see further.

IX. Track the celestial swan across a flawed glass while abbey bells bless some of us.

X.   What equation could describe her orbit? Will anyone ever catch my shine?

ELLEN RACHLIN

There Is Already Too Little Difference Between Living and Not

The problem is
slight shoulder twitches may be strikes
and no combination of kicks
will come from the same direction.
With careless speed, I circle sideways,
am forced to block.

The Grand Masters of martial arts,
the scholars of training whose
words and stares I took in
syllable by glare, now jumble
and knot as I seek an edge to win my fight.

Too easy to score on, I draw back.
Did they advise counter for each attack
or avoid? The Grand Masters are never
in the ring with me so why would
I react solely as they might direct?
Despite instincts inferior to their advice,
acting on instinct makes me feel like me.

Lessons in Remembering

YEHUDA AMICHAI

(Trans. Chana Bloch and Chana Kornfeld)

The School Where I Studied

I passed by the school where I studied as a boy
and said in my heart: here I learned certain things
and didn't learn others. All my life I have loved in vain
the things I didn't learn. I am filled with knowledge,
I know all about the flowering of the tree of knowledge,
the shape of its leaves, the function of its root system, its pests and parasites.
I'm an expert on the botany of good and evil,
I'm still studying it, I'll go on studying till the day I die.
I stood near the school building and looked in. This is the room
where we sat and learned. The windows of a classroom always open
to the future, but in our innocence we thought it was only landscape
we were seeing from the window.
The schoolyard was narrow, paved with large stones.
I remember the brief tumult of the two of us
near the rickety steps, the tumult
that was the beginning of a first great love.
Now it outlives us, as if in a museum,
like everything else in Jerusalem.

THOMAS DAVISON

The Forgotten Faces

The atmosphere in the prison classroom—you can cut it with the proverbial knife.
Students are edgy, scared. Only in the nursing homes is there more death.
Ten weeks into the term, on the verge of a spring they cannot see,
they learn their teacher will no longer be allowed back into the prison.

We see the virus victims on television: the important ones.
Less newsworthy, this classroom of stunned felons.
Forty-eight percent less recidivism for them, these students, versus the general
	prison population.

What will happen to them now? Painful, to have no answers.
Years of studying to achieve a GED, struggling to learn to read, to write,
to change a life—for them, everything is on hold now, even an online class.

It hurts, it isn't fair, why is this happening to me now?
The teacher-student relationship—this is all I have—please don't take it away.
You are the first male role model in my life; will we ever see each other again?
Makes me feel like crying, these faces of uncertainty.

LAUREN CAMP

Adult Basic Education

Just after noon, a man in a hat wide as a boat
comes floating alone
to the Tutoring Center. His eyes fall

to the floor, but his voice keeps rocking, rowing—
into the vast waters of his bipolar

dyslexic mind, the rough waters
                    of his ADD mind;
the Asperger current constantly tugging him down.

Pulling out his pencil case, he anxiously organizes lead.
Pulling off his hat, he tangles his hair. He tangles
his language, tying up

vowels and consonants until he is holding a line of strange sounds
and a net
that sifts every surface.

A fleet of students sails past, propelled
by an endless schedule of classes. The man

    is becoming submerged
is submerged
in himself in the thrall of his worry is submerged
in the sinking.

I lead him to a small room and close the door.
His words dart away.

He lays his hat
on the table as the island
of knowing drifts by. Sweat washes
his forehead.

Trawling each murky blue-brown word, his search
streams in all directions.

I am learning the limited scope of his course,
the slant reckoning of position,
and how we must both keep him buoyed.

To settle the speed, he gathers the sail
of his panic, opens his book

to this week's vocabulary words:
                     anecdote, appreciate, believe, condone.

He looks off along the bottom of his mind,
tells me again about Asperger's.

                "It's a form of optimism," he explains
and nerve cells miss the synapse:

he knows
what he means.

We begin riding the broad fin of language, finding our way
over the surface. We sound out
each alphabetical symbol: our C's crisp as fried kippers, each S extending
in curved lines down the coast of our tongues.

I say each word, and he hoists it up. I'm the one navigating
this trip because he's still leaving the harbor.
I'm the one tasked with pitching the rudder in the next logical direction.

Each word becomes a vessel
and we start to float
into the warm flow of paragraphs
in his *Sentence Skills* textbook. He's breathing better now.

When we've finished the hour, he's drained.
We've fished

                    for lost periods he can't always catch; we've angled
          for order, for every lesson in remembering.

Nothing is effortless, but we're both hooked
on language,

willing to sift deeper, and wash up again,

until, triumphant, we rise—

holding a word
or two

aloft.

LAUREN CAMP

Talking Twice

An eager teacher must learn the names of the many
timbred and mingled children: Araceli, Adriana,
even the remote Nazarena who sits off in the corner
with her lip in a pout and her braids near the floor.
You must climb the contrapuntal music and principles
of Spanish to the farms, to the border, to the everyday
significance of Roberto, Marisol, Xochie and Feros.
You must swallow each L, your tongue curling back
to extend the concert of sound; rake into the R's
and anchor these sonic eddying words to the dam
of your throat. To connect, you must caress
a language that won't hold in your mouth, must
arrange all that crowding and code. You must know
tortillas as life force, as kingdom; know *mole Colorado*
for the thick, steady spice and attack. Try to vanish
your measure, your prominent flatness, twist your
straight solemn words, make them glide and recline,
reduce slightly at corners. Somehow you must
comprehend *chicharrones,* when what you know
is onion rings swallowed at a diner on Elm Street.
You want to say nothing. After all, you are
the foreigner in this classroom of phonetic
exuberance. You are the one unpigmented, blank
and mundane, that exists on the outside of music.
But the boy with blue hair raises his hand. He asks
a question, and his palpable pitch fits the room. Yes,
your spirit is tired and coffee-taken, tight as the wind
thrown toward banded windows, yes, your accent's
all slaughtered and ordered, but you lift up your eyes.

This moment's important. You know the surface
of children is showy, and the underside more terrified.
And so, uncertain, you say words you don't trust:
transport and tilt them into each other, sustain,
and say them again, only louder. The language once
wild seems possible, hard on the outside but tunneling in.

SHERYL CLOUGH

Hopes for Novices

Like fur-bearing animals caught in leg-hold traps
your wary gazes pierce, avoid, glaze over—
what will happen when the traps are sprung?

I'll say to you, *Write.* When you confess
I didn't pass this course last term
I'll say *write about that. Write through that.*

Collaborative junk collectors,
we'll strip clichés for their parts
and rebuild prose engines to outrun Ferraris.

Verbs so active they incite riots
will lead revolts across blank pages.
Damn the comma splices, full speed ahead!

Nouns that dance like Northern Lights,
adjectives shimmering green phosphorescence,
similes startling as August avalanches:
all these create, and more.

Midway through the term when
one of you appears with purple streaks
blazed beneath your eyes and says,

My paper's late cuz I was in the hospital
my boyfriend gave me a concussion,
I'll say, *Write your heart across a page.*

Your blood and tears mix with ink
and because writers are alchemists first,
from the potion drink release.

Then in the calm before chaos, adjectives
jitterbug, adverbs do the two-step. Volumes
build, images collide with music, and
we triumph, yowling as a pack of wolves
across a once-silent chasm.

SALLY DAWIDOFF

The Trace of an Event

First Day of School. Nervous. Reread my notes, walking the long
blocks to the river. (Uptown, the sidewalks aren't that crowded;

still, head down, I nearly collided with a mailman. "*Watch* it!")
Scrapped my lesson plan & parroted Mr. Wilkinson instead.

If I've remembered it since junior high, an assignment must be good.
"On your way to school tomorrow," I told the students, "notice

everything you see." Goes nicely with their Summer Reading,
The Phantom Tollbooth: "The most important reason for going

from one place to another is to see what's in between." The book's
relentlessly didactic. But how lovely—"see what's in between."

Day 2. In they flocked from Recess in the cafeteria. (City life—
space is tight; no schoolyard.) I pictured them in Sheep Meadow,

sunlit, gamboling; felt bad. They wrote, & I took attendance (still
learning names). Then, one by one, they read aloud.

What they'd noticed on the way to school: *Narrow carpet on the stairs . . .*
The crossing guard . . . The sky . . . The blue sky . . . & the quiet girl:

I noticed my own body. One pipes up, "Sometimes my thoughts float away." "Mine too," I confess. The children look startled.

Day 3. At Recess, the Head convened an emergency faculty meeting in the auditorium, in the dark, a photo projected onto a screen.

I hurried to class. *Be reassuring.* The kids were restless. They'd been told; an older sibling had let it slip. *Keep them busy.*

"Who can think of an action verb?" "Bomb!" a girl calls out.

Parents came to claim their children. By three o'clock, just one remained (Alina? Elena?), doing homework at her desk.

Blue blue sky . . . My body . . .

Like a grown-up, I asked, "Dear, who's coming to get you?" Perhaps she didn't hear.

Frowning over her grammar, drawing diagrams. Smudged eyeglasses. Pink watchband. Brand-new yellow pencil going *Shhh.*

LISA FAY

Whittemore Library, Framingham State University

Because of a glitch in the brain,
I could not hear the buzzer
advising me to leave the library,
I was locked in my own world of books
keeping my imagination flowing and growing
soon to take me everywhere.
Since I was not a slave,
I did not have to prove I could
read and write, as Phillis Wheatley did.
Libraries were where August Wilson played hooky
all through high school,
tired of teachers
who doubted he could write
better than they could.
He got an A in absences.

PAUL HOSTOVSKY

Ninth Grade Vocabulary List

I put them all in alphabetical order—
apposite, betwixt, crenellated, duenna,
etcetera—on 8 x 5 index cards,
with their definitions on the back
in etymological order, and studied them
all alone in my room. But in order
to own them, to internalize them,
to be able to retrieve them at the drop
of a word, I knew I needed to use them,
to say them, to embed them in
my sentences. "Please pass the friable,
crenellated chicken pot pie betwixt
the sweet potatoes and green beans,
duenna," I said to my mother
at dinner. She looked over her shoulder
and winced as though I'd fired a volley
of vocabulary over her head, nicking
her earlobe, embedding itself in the wall
like shrapnel. There's no getting around it,
the big words are intimidating, formidable,
redoubtable, apposite and sometimes
the opposite of apposite. But a hairless,
feckless, rangy kid who didn't know
how to fight and didn't have a girlfriend
could use them to good advantage
to parley, and to parlay, and at parties
to impress girls, blow his rivals away.

PAUL HOSTOVSKY

Writing Platypuses

A platitude and a platypus
have one thing in common:
their first syllable,
which comes from the Greek
for flat. The resemblance
ends there. Because a platitude,
which is sometimes referred to
as a cliché, is nothing like
a platypus, which is sometimes referred to
as the duck-billed platypus.
Bill of a duck, tail of a beaver, feet
of an otter. The platypus
is no platitude. It's an original—
the sole living representative
of its family and genus. Write
platypuses, undergraduates. Be
original, be surprising. Be
the venomous mammal that lays eggs,
figuratively speaking, whenever
you speak or write. Don't be flat
or trite like a platitude. Be the flat-
footed platypus, body so genuine
that early European scientists
thought it was a fake—several animals
sewn together. For your first
writing assignment, don't be all
you can be. Be everything you aren't.
Be sphinxian and alive for once
in your life. One page. Due Friday at 5.

MAJOR JACKSON

Winter

The boughs have been naked for weeks.
Snowplows scrape the highway clean of its sugar.
People withdraw into their nests and study
the language of fire. A group of high school girls
on their way home in the afternoon dark
falls into an embankment and flaps their arms
and legs as though cloud-swimming toward the coming world.
The blank silence of dead earth forces us
to gaze up, harvest the black music that belongs
to all in the eyes of the future who will turn to the spheres
and study too whatever light to fill their emptiness.

SCOTT LOWERY

Shawn

Hennepin County Home School, 1987

My first and only year there,
that heavy clump of keys
holstered at my hip—
I tried to show them what
anyone should know: how to read
a tape and cut cheap pine
to a squared-off line, thinking I suppose
that accuracy and luck
could buy them different lives.
He was tall and caught on fast,
able to give me his attention
like a small gift as long as *they*
could show *me* how to pop a car lock.
"You know you could build things
for money," I'd say, and he'd ask
"What's that pay?" then smirk
at my inflated guess.
None of us were leaving
any time soon, so I'd laugh too.
We hung drywall, the dust like flour
on their brown hands. We drilled holes,
pulled nails, my tradesman tricks
blooming like parking lot weeds
there in the classroom's bright
optimistic buzz. Maybe he asked
"Can I try that?" or else
just smiled and the next day
showed another kid,
"Hold it here, like this."

Later, he got his grades and
circled back to the Near North Side,
the weeks crossed off and done.
I still see him, eye to eye,
taking his crew down the corridor
toward a lukewarm dinner.
"All right, Lowery." "All right, Shawn."
That summer, he was waiting in a car
for somebody. The bullet ran its
small, precise course through
his head, fixing his age
for my *Star Tribune*. Next day,
no update or remembrances,
just a new day,
another card in a crooked deck.
I kept teaching, twenty years
measured in fractions of hope.
Every fall, his is
a face I look for,
lifting itself grudgingly,
generously
up toward mine.

SCOTT LOWERY

Field Trip to Chair City

Gardner, Massachusetts, 1985

Gears grinding Elm Street morning quiet
into diesel fumes, our school bus
bounces us on past the famous
Giant Chair, a twenty-foot high ladderback
that still commemorates how commerce
won that second Revolution,
its red brick mills surmounting
every rock-strewn river
from here to the White Mountains

then lets us out at one of the last few
not yet gone south, where we follow
through a dusty dream of corridors,
watch infeed and outfeed, flashing lights,
machines imported from the future
squeezed, it seems by magic, into
horse-drawn spaces,
                              my kids with just
their crisp jean jackets rolled
studiously up skinny forearms,
a couple bucks for lunch,
the cocky walk of some
familial millwright or factory hand—
they joke, nudge, refuse to ask
the good questions we've written down,
shrugging off each older
spitting image of themselves

until we all fall silent
around the bandsaw man—

straight-backed and intent beneath
the whir of a huge cast iron wheel,
he slices out the curves
of arm, crest, rocker,
all drawn by tradition but cut
by him alone behind the saw,
hard maple stacked six high and flying
past the blade like bread in someone's
crazy bakery,

scraps clattering in a pile
at the feet of these wide-eyed kids,
	sons of truckers,
	daughters of drunks,
surprised in this moment of then
meets now, suspended,
crossing our fingers,

we watch as pencil line gets swallowed
by the blurred, unflinching blade,
as wood comes open, shows its hidden
face then falls away on both sides
while the parts pile up,
	half dozen by half dozen,
blank and unfinished as real lives.

AIMEE NEZHUKUMATATHIL

On Listening to Your Teacher Take Attendance

Breathe deep even if it means you wrinkle
your nose from the fake-lemon antiseptic

of the mopped floors and wiped-down
doorknobs. The freshly soaped necks

and armpits. Your teacher means well,
even if he butchers your name like

he has a bloody sausage casing stuck
between his teeth, handprints

on his white, sloppy apron. And when
everyone turns around to check out

your face, no need to flush red and warm.
Just picture all the eyes as if your classroom

is one big scallop with its dozens of icy blues
and you will remember that winter your family

took you to the China Sea and you sank
your face in it to gaze at baby clams and sea stars

the size of your outstretched hand. And when
all those necks start to crane, try not to forget

someone once lathered their bodies, once patted them
dry with a fluffy towel after a bath, set out their clothes

for the first day of school. Think of their pencil cases
from third grade, each full of sharp pencils, a pink pearl eraser.

Think of their handheld pencil sharpener and its tiny blade.

NAOMI SHIHAB NYE

Separation Wall

When the milk is sour,
it separates.

The next time you stop speaking,
ask yourself why you were born.

They say they are scared of us.
The nuclear bomb is scared of the cucumber.

When my mother asks me to slice cucumbers,
I feel like a normal person with fantastic dilemmas:

Do I make rounds or sticks? Shall I trim the seeds?
I ask my grandmother if there was ever a time

she felt like a normal person every day,
not in danger, and she thinks for as long

as it takes a sun to set and says, Yes.
I always feel like a normal person.

They just don't see me as one.
We would like the babies not to find out about

the failures waiting for them. I would like
them to believe on the other side of the wall

is a circus that just hasn't opened yet. Our friends,
learning how to juggle, to walk on tall poles.

TONY REEVY

View from the Disputanta School
1975

The junior high window—panes
and metal strips, peeling paint, dead
flies, chips of caulk—frames
the ebony train rolling past

from mountains to the ships
at Norfolk. Bored by algebra,
I hear the whistle, the roar;
look; count *one, two, three* and on,
sometimes well past a hundred.

The cars, each black, blazoned
N&W, Virginian,
trailed by small clouds of
coal dust, ballast dirt.

Beyond the tracks,
I see the green swamps
of Southside—unlike
the trains, never moving

except when a tree at the edge
crashes down, logged.
To the boy in the room,
the sight is beautiful.

MILLER OBERMAN

This and That at The Frick

I bring my students to the Frick to see Frank
O'Hara's beloved "Polish Rider" and after giggling
at the work Bronzino did on the silver painted crotch
of "Lodovico Capponi," whose silk sprouts like a big
snail or scrolled bedpost between his legs, we walk to the West Gallery
and all agree Rembrandt did a grand job. The young man is handsome,
his horse handsomer, especially its head. The rider
looks like he could dismount, meet O'Hara and
Ashbery at the San Remo or Cedar for drinks.
I get it. But across the hall, El Greco's "Vincenzo Anastagi,"
despite every frippery draws no titters.
Graying at the temples, he is armored at the chest and arms,
with a white ruffle around his neck. It escapes
his sleeves, too, bloomy as the rind of stinky cheese,
or egg whites whipped to stiff peaks.
Against this froth his uncultivated face, mid-length
beard, dark eyes, maybe kind, maybe sad. The green
velvet of impossibly puffy shorts does nothing
to lighten the weight of his eyes, nor does cloth
billowing behind him, a drapery from nowhere
come to hold him in relief. A color I can't name. Not
red, not purple or brown. Like blood in a dream,
oiled as bone broth. What a strange word,
"relief," which used to denote the body
of a dead person or any kind of remains, but now
means ease, deliverance from pain, or the impression,
in art, that a thing is raised above a surface. Vincenzo
is all these things at once, and I can't wait to bring Louisa here—
Louisa, who this morning on the train said *gross*, reading

over my shoulder O'Hara's description of
"laborers" who "feed their dirty / glistening torsos."
Gross, she said, on the B train going over the bridge,
meaning O'Hara's reduction of these toilers to objectified
working class trunks, and she was right, they're never
just beautiful, these old things, these men's things.

CATHERINE WOODARD

Gettysburg

Gen. Daniel Sickles takes his amputated
leg home in a barrel of whiskey. Takes
credit for the Union victory
when Lincoln visits three days later.

Rep. Sickles (D-NY) works the missing leg
more skillfully than the one attached.
Nominates himself for a Medal of Honor,
hitched to a bill to hallow Gettysburg—

where he sent 10,000 New York boys—
against orders—down from Cemetery Ridge
to a peach orchard, to slaughter by the Rebs.
On the 150th anniversary of the battle,

two sweaty brothers squirm on Little Round Top
in midday sun, oblivious to parents, tour guide.
They wear blue Union caps, struggle
to attach plywood bayonets to replica rifles.

JENNIFER SCHNEIDER

Fill in the Blanks

Crisp lined white paper, wide-ruled
filler paper, college-lined loose leaf
piles, too. Carefully placed on desks
in neatly organized stacks.

Airs and heirs. Assessments,
assignments, and assumptions.

No. 2s up. Heads down.
Ready. Set. Go. You may begin.
Deceptively clean, clear, and simple.

Teachers read
pre-printed instructions.
Children wrestle
with pre-historic presumptions.

Fill in the blanks
of eight
neatly organized squares.
Symmetry meets mystery.

All sides the same.
Appropriate structures long assumed
and preordained.

A dearth of triangles.
Octagons and trapezoids, too.

Each grid demands
a simple fact. Low stakes
at the base of Bloom's
hierarchy.

Fill-in-the-blank routines round
out mornings
made of mac 'n' cheese leftovers,
missed alarms, and public
transportation mazes.

Listen carefully. Follow
all rules. Stay within
all lines. Ready. Set. Go.

Identify by name.
Write legibly.
Mind your grammar.

Mother.
Father.
Space for one.
Siblings.
Two lines.
Pets. Three.

Simple concepts
captured in eight-
and-a-half by eleven
sheets
that tear
down the middle

as students seek
to comply
with rulers
of worlds
unknown.

SORAYA SHALFOROOSH

Education Has No Borders

That bus stuck in mud and blood.
Malala and her friends.
The sounds of girls chatting
turning to screams in seconds.

We all know what came next—
hospitals, the airlift.
That couldn't stop her.
No ignorance, no bullets
could stop her quest.

Shift to drive—remark at how we are here
years later, Malala the activist
empowering not just Swat Valley,
not just Pakistan, but all of us.
I hear her voice, powerful and clear.
On school buses, in classrooms, on TVs
around the globe.

We are her students.

SORAYA SHALFOROOSH / DYLAN YAHIAOUI

Asynchronous Learning During the Pandemic, Week One

Middle School shut, Social Studies and English combined into one class.
And my son must pick from a list of inspirational leaders to write about.
Malala, he says. *Because people don't know what other people go through*
      to get educated.
People should focus on what they have instead of what they lack.
It was so sad she got shot. It's not her fault at all.
And she, she spoke out, she spoke out after suffering to help others.
She gave me hope too. Here studying alone, with dyslexia and ADD and
if a girl about my age did what she did to learn, then I can do my best to learn.
I can get through this. "Education first," Malala says.
No bullet, no boundaries can defeat her wisdom.

Ancestral Spirits

JOEL ALLEGRETTI

Lot's Wife

Do you know Bera? He was the king of Sodom.
And Abram? My husband's uncle.
Do you remember my name? Of course not.
You don't recall what no one bothered to record.
I will tell you my name is Bad Girl. Wife Who Must
Be Disciplined. Woman Who Doesn't Know Her Place.
I served my man faithfully. Scrubbing the floors.

Picking sand from the lentils. Roasting the lamb
Until the sputtering fat raised blisters on my hands.
Breaking my back carrying the water jars.
Bearing his children. But he was the righteous one.
The good one. Who thrust his daughters before the city's
Preening queens. Who believed their virtue less costly
Than an angel's backside. Listen. We *all* were Sodomites.

While cattle licked and eroded my haunches,
The apples of their father's eye dulled him with wine,
Then had their turns with him to continue the line.
What could come but a race of drooling, slope-browed idiots?
As for me? Know that I *am* the salt of the earth;
But as far as you or anyone is concerned, I'm fit only
For seasoning the wreckage and bones of the damned.

KIM ADDONIZIO

Creased Map of the Underworld

Nothing is so beautiful as death,
thinks Death: stilled lark on the lawn,
its twiggy legs drawn up, squashed blossoms
of skunks and opossums on the freeway,
dog that drags itself trembling down
the front porch step, and stops
in a black-gummed grimace
before toppling into the poppies.
The ugly poppies. In Afghanistan
they are again made beautiful
by a mysterious blight. Ugly
are the arriving American soldiers, newly shorn
and checking their email,
but beautiful when face-up in the road
or their parts scattered
like bullet- or sprinkler-spray
or stellar remains. Lovely
is the nearly expired star
casting its mass into outer space,
lovelier the supernova
tearing itself apart
or collapsing like Lana Turner
in Frank O'Hara's poem.
Nothing is so beautiful as a poem
except maybe a nightingale,
thinks the poet writing about death,
sinking Lethe-wards. Lovely river
in which the names are carefully entered.
In this quadrant are the rivers of grief and fire.

Grid north. Black azimuth.
Down rivers of *Fuck you*s and orchids
steer lit hearts in little boats
gamely making their way,
spinning and flaming, flaming
and spiraling, always down—
down, the most beautiful of the directions.

DESIRÉE ALVAREZ

Botanical Drawing of Colonialism

You—poppy, launching ships. You Helen of a bloom.
What is it to be a flower? *Papaver somniferum.*

Ancient and current fields of war flowers, poppies
tended and harvested by the poorest.

Old story, centuries of opium wars, kingdoms
controlling peasants. All the brown hands

stirring vats of sticky sap all day.
The harvest drugging generations

in the sleep of oblivion. The same flower
growing in the backyard of my childhood.

Poppy, flower of my mother.
I remember her in the garden,

tending to their pink crepe ballets.
But whirling at the center,

black cave of Morpheus
where she disappeared at the end

in surrender to the witch's field.
Neolithic opiate flower,

making and re-making yourself over again.
The best cure for pain.

Bouquet of anemone for my mother,
a spray of bleeding heart for my mother,

bloodroot sanguinaria that used to grow
along her path. *Papaveracea*, you are all

descendants of Demeter's flower.
O tiny purple windflower, withstanding gale,

valiant like my mother who soldiered on as we all do,
even the plants, until we can no longer.

In the library of the Botanical Garden in Brooklyn
I learn heroin is named for giving heroes their bravery.

On Veterans Day I plant coral poppies
thinking not of soldiers or my mother,

but of the teens lost to the spell
of addiction in the next town over.

I keep planting you to make myself over.
To begin and end with beauty.

Ancient poppy queen raising her arms
to the sky blackened with ashes of goddess.

ELLEN BASS

Goat, Cow, Man

After the mob murdered the man for eating
a cow, it was found to be meat
from a goat. Why can I not
stop thinking about it—
the stringy flesh inside his gut,
and the microbes run riot when his heart
stopped—how fast they started
breaking down the blood-clotted
muscle of his stomach, slick intestines,
as though they were meant
to destroy the evidence of human—what
can I call it? sin? the curse of certainty? some twist
in the helix that insists on splitting
us apart?—the cow is not the goat. I am not
you. The man is a few inches of old newsprint,
a knot of hair, eye sockets,
but I keep picturing that
kitchen, his wife and children stuttering,
it's goat, it's goat,
and the goat, her white
coat, the little kernels of her teeth,
her pale slitted eyes.

LAUREN CAMP

Fairy Tales with Girls

Here's what I know:
most girls believe in the color turquoise
in great detail, and the echo

of that color. Some believe in wishes.
The two in the corner:
their eyes are always open too wide.

Their smiles plop on the dry landscape
of the carpeted room.
Other girls are hitch and muster.

I dwell on them,
and those still drifting.
Chew slowly on their many words.

We have dirt and paint
under our nails. Hours breathe
on us as we write characters

and tempers, each side of myth
and privacy. I let them decide
their dignity and sadness.

In one fairy tale, a whiskered cat;
in another, unicorns. We're still working
on our villains, giving them names.

SHERYL CLOUGH

What Raven Said

Grand Geyser of Yellowstone, October 1998

See my color. The indigo that lies
within the black, the purple.

Note the perfection of my every feather,
how each fits the next without break.

Find the downy wisps covering the notch
at the base of my beak.

Feel my beak, strong and sleek.
With it, I   talk   sing   chant.
Through it, I drink crystal mountain water,
suck guts of field mice and sweet pulp
of berries plucked from heathered hillsides.
I pick puffs of down, sticks, and shiny bits
that strike my fancy, all for the nest.

From my beak, I dropped the great clamshell
giving birth to your race.

See the flash in my eye, meteor in glass,
the light of inner world to guide you.
When your eyes perceive perfection
can your heart lag far behind?
Your heart pumps molten blood to melt
the fear caged within concrete ribs.

You know you want to fly. Practice daily clucks
and trills. With your mouth wide open,
snag juicy beetles from tall grass
to nourish those arms you flap

against an unbelieving breeze. Pad your nest
with feathers and fluff gathered in the wild.
Fix sundown eyes to the fiery horizon, and gaze

until the blaze becomes you.

RUTH DANON

The Ruins

pools of water over pitted stones
      near Ghilarza where
I came late
      to the moment
of revelation
      the woman teaching
said "a grave"
said all were once alike in the huge pit
men and women and children
in the same place
      even dogs
were buried together
      until invaders, men,
built towers with circular stairs
      (I did not climb)

      and after the towers it was
everyone interred
      alone in death

        **

walking away I saw
coming towards me, ewes and their lambs
in the rare grass
bells at their necks, ringing
a new story

ANNIE FINCH

Brave Women's Amulet

Women have voices it's time to believe in.
Brave women's words, spoken out clear and steady,
move us through generous ways of achieving.
Women have voices it's time to believe in,
braiding sweet worlds. This grave, loving weaving
is singing our lives back, and women are ready—
women have voices. It's time to believe in
brave women's words, spoken out clear and steady.

ANNIE FINCH

Moon for Our Daughters

Moon that is linking our daughters'
Choices, and still more beginnings,
Threaded alive with our shadows,

These are our bodies' own voices,
Powers of each of our bodies,
Threading, unbroken, begetting

Flowers from each of our bodies,
These are our spiraling borders
Carrying on your beginnings,

Chaining through shadows to daughters,
Moving beyond our beginnings,
Moon of our daughters, and mothers.

TESS GALLAGHER

Redwing

The readers of poetry, the writers of
poetry. Nation inside
the nation. The rainbow holding briefly over
the Strait of Juan de Fuca, its violet
inner rim, its guess-work dome
of crimson. My back to the sun for this
to happen at all, the eye extending
its shadow until it sees into
what it doesn't see. I don't have to think
of raindrops hanging as light, or to command
the schoolbook corpses of refraction and
internal reflection to be dazzled. The myth
of the Vilela Indians, its rainbow
a gigantic serpent charmed
by a small girl until it sheds her
sway and piecemeal ravages the world, vanquished
at last by an army of birds—that's good enough
for me. And victory too, each bird
dipping itself in the blood
of the monster.

RACHEL HADAS

February 29, 2020

As if we knew but didn't know we knew.
February 29: Leap Day,
an extra day, an ordinary day,
predictable even in being extraordinary—
a bonus day in the old dispensation
we couldn't guess was close to termination.
When did we start to sense the great subtraction?

Leap Day, the. And I was on my way
to catch a train to go to Tarrytown
(people still had a schedule and a plan,
mapping the hours to their destination)
to run a four-hour class on poetry—
specifically, tailored to the day,
on poems that performed a lyric leap:
the way the mind hopscotches, A to C
or D or Z, a little lateral hop
or skip, a sudden swerve, a syncopation.

I waited for the train. Grand Central Station:
tourists and travelers in circulation,
all of them aimed at some desired location,
throngs chatting, texting, pausing to gaze up
at the iconic ceiling's constellations.
A pregnant woman in a scarlet coat
posed for a photo with a selfie stick.
Her baby must be six months old by now.

Waiting for my train, could I foresee
crowds would soon be prohibited by law?
Could anyone imagine the great hall

would within weeks be scoured clean of all
humanity? Just dust motes in the sun.
Idle tracks. An empty waiting room.
Whoever sensed it didn't want to see.

That extra day, that ordinary day,
I got where I was going on the train
and taught the lyric leap, as per the plan;
then, tired, happy, bathed in poetry,
caught a train and travelled back again,
retraced my steps. Grand Central one more time.
Maybe make that Grand Central one last time.

Looking back now, I can see I saw,
that Leap Day when we leaped with poetry,
the cold blue morning light, the dappled sky,
the river silver grey as we rode by.
But what no one was prepared to see:
not quite a harbinger, since it was there
already. No, a searchlight raked the air
invisibly, masked by the morning's glare.

That searchlight still is circling everywhere,
and everyone's a target—you and me.
And yet with the bewilderment and fear,
upheaval on a scale we scarcely see
even though we sense it in the air,
something else persists invisibly,
companion to our stunned anxiety—
something that isn't going anywhere.
Poetry is still here.

RICK HILLES

To Disenchantment

I praise the hoax exposed, the sham in shambles.
    The huckster's smirk, and the illusionist's oops!
    And when a clown pie lands in the right face.
I praise the scam that scrams, the jilted lover
    who disregards the teleprompters and clearly
    goes for broke as they cut to an infomercial.
And I praise that I'm not even tempted to be sold.
But if I were, please throw a very wet sock at me!

I praise the sunset that moves behind a cloud.
    And the grass that Whitman loved, even if
    Joseph Brodsky *was* right: it *is* propaganda.
(Forgive me, Uncle Walt—I know that's not what
    you meant—but what for you was a "uniform
    hieroglyph" is now *a DDT-refined tautology*.)
I praise those who walk back others' tantrums
    clearly lying when they say they were joking.
And I even praise all nascent immune systems
    that need our germs to realize themselves.
And bright ideas revealed in fun-house mirrors.

I praise the delayed romance to drive up ratings.
The shamelessly sleazy ad campaign. The easy
    to spot out rhetoric of church and state.
I praise those who are equally unconvinced that
    we'll ever know what happened in our lifetimes.

And I praise the unlovely fragrance it all exudes,
    revealing just enough for us to know ourselves.

And I praise (almost!) the evidence that never comes.
All bunk defunct, and every ballyhooer removed.
And I praise the lofty and mossy prognostications
    and their equally lofty and mossy prognosticators.

And I even salute the red-lipped truth, which
    eludes me, especially when I seek it most.
Even if it exists as the song of an extinct bird,
    to which nothing we've heard even compares.
Or conjures one iota of its allure or ecstatic majesty.

And so I praise what at once raises my red flags.
Even the cringe-worthy salesman's "Trust me!"
But I will honor the first man, woman, or child
    who approaches me without cunning or guile
    or subterfuge of any kind to say something
I've never heard before, even something about
    the grass, bringing it to me with both hands,
    asking, "Hey, Mister! Do *you* know what this is?"
And I will praise how far we're willing to go to see
    the grass together, as through a microscope
    so that the fire in every cell ignites us too!!

RICK HILLES

To Misunderstanding

On the radio today, a neurologist identified
                the most important capacity
                                of the human brain
                as being its capacity to contemplate
a self beyond itself. Even the interviewer was not so sure
                he understood what his guest just said
                when he asked the specialist to explain it all again.

I was not sure how the man would make his point again
                so with thousands, I imagine tens of thousands
                                invisibly listening
                along with me—we all leaned in, like silence itself
to the radio voice who then told us all about the brain's
                plasticity—he had doubted it himself, he said—
for many years, decades, really; he'd heard a colleague

assert the theory thirty years or so before. "A crank"
                who he knew now had been a visionary all along
                                and led him to the realization
                that he'd been wrong about all he'd known about
the brain. Being able to see beyond one's earlier position, that
                point of view, was the key that freed him
                to reject each former hypothesis that he'd maintained.

This was the brain, at any age—making new connections.
                And to abandon old neural connections for new
                                pathways seemed the very
                hallmark of consciousness and our humanity.

But how many of us ever really see past a prior understanding?
And abandon it completely? This man
of science moved me most when he finally admitted

how wrong he'd been—in every other hypothesis
he'd made. Moving unknowingly from error
to error, without a sense of
progress is what made him become himself—
even if all our work seems like nothing but the sum of all our errors—
it will have been good to share our work, nevertheless.
A life may fail to yield even one answer and still be well spent.

JANE HIRSHFIELD

In a Former Coal Mine in Silesia

In a former coal mine in Silesia, a thousand feet inside the earth,
a tongue kept speaking.

In the Arctic, by the triangular door to the Svalbard seed vault,
a tongue almost fearless, almost not clumsy, spoke.
Spoke verbs, conjunctions, adjectives, adverbs, nouns.

In a small town in the Australian Outback,
in the city of Nanjing, near a gate still recalling unthinkable closures,
by a lake in Montana, a tongue almost steady,
almost not stumbling, spoke facts, hypotheses, memories, riddles, stories.

Lungs accept their oxygen without trembling.
Feet stand inside their foot shapes, inside shoes someone has sewn.

We close the eyes of the dead so they will not see their not-seeing.
Light falls on the retinas' stubbornness, on pupils refusing to turn toward or away.

Fireflies, furnaces, quicksilvers fill them, cities & forests glinting though already
finished.

And the tongues, the faithless tongues, continue speaking,
as lovers will, because they still love, long past the hour there is nothing left to say.

CYNTHIA HOGUE

The Bite of the Apple

1.

In the backyard the apple tree had a dignity the child never thought twice about I mean why would she question what was always a given? It was tall, shading the whole yard, its fruit sweet and freely she ate and freely climbed. From the highest bough she could reach the garage roof in one direction and in the other her sister's upstairs nursery. If she stretched she might touch the window's glass like God or fall like Lucifer. Years later the girl biked with her sister to an orchard to pick apples as it happened for the last time they felt at ease in their bodies untouched by power. Soaring past waving fields, they glowed in the lucent fall. Small were the clouds the golden cumulus that day but firm their place in the wider sky.

2.

Like the cumulus the small woman however touched as a girl by power affirmed herself before a wide congress of stares in the name of truth though accused of accusing one of the Elect, who himself when before the tribunal sneered in outrage I'm sure sincerely after all no other woman had dared name him but she from his own class and race and save for gender the privilege he'd been born into which is to say for her a more provisional version. She'd harmed him he said for good. *I liked beer I still like beer* he repeated to make a point he seemed to think clear. The woman accused of accusing spoke softly in a high voice because she was she said afraid to speak up, but her words made evident the strength no one had bent, the dignity none could tar. The woman had in essence picked the apple the man then asserted for himself. His alone to eat. Thereafter would he abide himself as an apple abides the mouth. As the core the teeth.

STEPHEN MASSIMILLA

After the Ritual of Descent

I.

Down from my widower's roof walk,

I've picked up potsherds
of a crypted language, burnt wicks under moth wings,
vein bits in chips of rock.

                         Clawing through wet mud
toward higher ground,
uncoiling in concurrent torso-warp, Anubis unleashes
interlocking howls.

                    To the awkward rhythm of bird-taps

on the tarp, that bellowing brings back Buster:
Paw prints of the beast that once guarded my lone flank

pock the incline.

II.

The Greater Past leaned into the living
leaves; an avalanche of wind

washed out my encampment. Sad wolves
of frayed fibers, slow-moving smoke waves.

My animal blood in the Great Below, I was huddled
between our Cross and our Menorah, branches

trampled a thousand times over. Heavier raps
on the door shut to the dark

and the blow of the thunderbolt
that swallowed the five-mile-high night

when the barking returned and the brutal hussars
entered private quarters

of dread, pulling the threads

of a tear
from the horrified eyelid.

III.

Something deeper than fear comes back
after that: a snuffling, as of an illegal hog
tracking dirt-rich truffles

on a forbidden estate

or a hint too subtle to be sensed
in time:

a lick of onyx salt, sheer cliff,
the myth coming right to the brink.

JENNY MOLBERG

Loving Ophelia Is

loving a ghost and loving a ghost is loving yourself
and loving yourself is a sudden sorrow
and a sudden sorrow is the place where the river pools
and the place where the river pools is not suicide and
not suicide is confronting the unknown and confronting
the unknown is the active condition of womanhood
and the active condition of womanhood is the beauteous nature
of Denmark and the beauteous nature of Denmark is lovesickness
and lovesickness is obsession with a version of yourself
and obsession with a version of yourself is egomania and egomania
is a room of mirrors and a room of mirrors is love and hate simultaneously
and love and hate simultaneously is the trick of abuse
and the trick of abuse is a vexation of the mind and
a vexation of the mind is the feeble dawn of gaslight and tea
and the feeble dawn of gaslight and tea is an overbearing husband
and an overbearing husband is a soliloquy of clichés and a soliloquy
of clichés is the misery of scholars and the misery of scholars
is an old friend's skull and an old friend's skull is a sudden sorrow
and a sudden sorrow is holding one's breath
and holding one's breath is swimming away and swimming away
is the other shore on which Ophelia has woken

ELLEN RACHLIN

The Invention of Dance

We don't know their names—
the ones that discovered
when bathed in notes
pushed through swan
bone flutes that limbs float.

Were they inspired by life
or the sparseness of prayer,
needing a miracle to offer for miracle?

Not only are we here,
but whenever the music
is right we move in our own ways—
owning the gaits—
the threes, fours,
circles, squares, dips,
and breath that can etch
an arc in the spine
even if just balancing in thought

for one may need to find
a reason to dance to
the moon in blackened night—
so, within each is choreo
to pull darkness away
and from soul
a shimmering light until
spirit takes leave,
shimmying with grace.

ELAINE SEXTON

Landscape with Power Lines

The twisting chords no longer
bother me. As I see it,
they heighten the light, halved

and halved again, leaves and clouds, snow
and storm. The breeze moves an olive branch
over one line, then another below. Each branch

acts as if her leaves aren't about to be swayed
to stay on one side for good. They remain
undecided. Today they are subject to dust

kicked up as a truck hauling crops powers past.
Birds make their wild plans to nest
one last time. They weave their sticks

and tissue their housing
including these lines.
We are bound to live together.

LAURA TOHE

Kinaaldá

The east slowly floods with yellow light. Nalí stops my flow of sleep.
It's time.

I slip into red moccasins. Smooth my hair and shield.
It's time.

Emerging from my cocoon, eidetic memory stirs the crossing by rainbow.
It's time.

"Create strength inside you," Nalí says. Released, I meet the sun full-on above
prairie dog holes.
It's time

to shed my chrysalis of girlhood in the shimmering heat.
It's time

to run towards the house of *Beauty;* it's time to run towards eternity.
It's time

to become
White Shell Woman.

YUYUTSU SHARMA

Running Out of Ink

Running out of ink
given my karma to pen down

my grief as death rages
in the dark vaults of the world

and poison is sprinkled
with glee on my people

trapped in dog cages, beaten,
broken like stones in enclosed spaces

of hatred, abused and maimed
as their children cry out,

gasping for breath,
their journeys to reach distant homes

thwarted, mocked,
their efforts to survive declared

uncouth and unconstitutional
by well-fed anchors sitting

on plush sofas
in the studios of current anarchy.

His giant potter's wheel plops out
piles of corpses, rightful relics of wrath.

In my dream last night
I saw a blue Mediterranean shore crop up

in my backyard, a sudden sight
of joy at this grim hour.

From my rooftop
I see crystal waves crashing against mossy walls

of my ancestral house in Punjab
where once wheat fields stretched

to the rim of summer songs
of wailing hoopoes.

Life multiplies here in my village,
even nails of the corpses flung into

the bottomless wells
a decade before my birth

grow nonstop along with their black
shiny hair, eyelashes and long lush beards.

"The women were so beautiful,
kohl-eyed, fair and sharp-featured, houris,"

my grandma once
confided in my childhood,

"Death," she said, "is a discarded broom
of gloom, a misshapen pygmy slur."

The Queen Mother in her tales cried so much
when the father of my hero, the king, brought in another wife

that she lost her eyesight
from crying all the time.

And Grandpa whispered the anecdotes
of darker times when the British ruled.

The floods swamped the entire district,
everyone waded knee-deep in the muddy waters

and corpses of the animals
came floating to our doors, instead of singing saints.

On the seventh day, he slept
in the main baithak of our house,

uttering prayers as the water kept rising
ready to cross our threshold

and the thunder roared
overhead all night long.

In the early hours of the dawn
he dreamed of the waters rushing back

to the colossal mouth of the blue-throated god,
and life resuming its normal pace.

He woke out of his creaking cot
moved out of the house to step on the ground

dry as the bones
of our ancestral spirits.

ALINA STEFANESCU

Aubade with Caged Animals
For P.

I leave you all the worries
of money, oil change, dental floss,
frozen soup, clean masks.

Even the gorilla nightmare
is yours
if you want her,
if you have a place

to keep her
when she busts loose
from the Birmingham Zoo.

Hasn't it always been
about escaping
or leaving
or dying
without wounding

the watchers?

Dreams taste like pennies,
I think sometimes
fear, blood, terror,
history,

all those cusps

taste similar
when swallowed
or tendered
inside us.

ALINA STEFANESCU

To Muffin from the Mountainous Molehill

They let the lizard go near
a drain pipe; four kids crouched
round the motion of freedom,

or what it resembles of
rambling. Blessed be that.
And blessed be she who

comes in the name of the Birmingham Zoo's
forlornest lion, his paws raw from pacing the cage.
I know, I know *zoos are for children*,

or preservation of exotic foreign
species. I'm telling you this due to that
which I mentioned from the peak

of my mountainous molehill.
You are laboring for money and status
while I work for nothing greater

than *thanks*, that divine never-
forthcomingness. This is the age of outraging
outrage. Be kind to customers who expect

to buy respect like aspirin. Red peppers
exacerbate heartburn. Angina is everywhere
now. Bless. *Stoop down and drink and live,*

a voice said. Its inflections the color of
catnip, the behold of wild violets, the lark-
spur's rainbow-riddling tongue.

The lizard is loose, pumpkin. Blessed
be the inviolable escaping from kingdoms
reliant on quiet captives.

MICHAEL WATERS

One Caw

Against the snow they're silhouettes,
These crows, how many hundreds
Burdening branches, these
Blunt-scissors-&-construction-paper
Kindergarten cutouts, these
Rorschach blots, sloppy calligraphy,
Or jagged wounds, the sky torn,
But not political, if that's possible.
Then a blast scatters the murder
& any direction they flee is wrong.
Smoke on the hillside. The soldier
Stares, rifle tensed on one shoulder.
He's looking me over, wondering who I am.
I've seen this scene in films, Russian novels,
Old Master oils, Pathé newsreels.
Or on CNN—smoke in the city,
Schoolchildren scattered among rubble—
If that's possible—or blue sky, shade trees,
Suburban sprawl. The police car stops.
The boy stares. How many hundreds.
One caw, then silence.
Something horrible about to happen.

MICHAEL WATERS

Electric Fence

For my son, 10, in the first year of the presidency of Donald Trump

He dared me to touch my finger to the fence,
The fence which we'd been warned against.
Its wire whining mutely sparked my fingertip.
And he recalled the science teacher's lesson
About current and conduction, so
Grasped my hand and squinched his lids
As I prodded the wire once more.
We yelped as the splinter of lightning
Tore through my limbs into his.
Four cows, eyeing us, drooled deep indifference.
Next he coaxed his reluctant mom
To affix herself to this human chain . . .
Now the electricity needled us,
Stitching red thread through all three of us,
And could have leapt cross-country
Citizen to citizen unstoppably,
But instead fused fast the DNA
Of our stricken—and still smoldering—family.

INDEX OF CONTRIBUTORS

Addonizio, Kim, 123, 190

Alexander, Carol, xvii, 4, 5

Alexander, Elizabeth, 33, 124

Allegretti, Joel, 189

Alvarez, Desirée, 3, 192

Alyan, Hala, 35, 38

Amichai, Yehuda, 155

Bass, Ellen, 34, 126

Betts, Reginald Dwayne, 40, 41

Bolina, Jaswinder, 42, 128

Brenner, Rosalind, 44

Camp, Lauren, 157, 160, 195

Cane, Tina, 46, 130

Cavalieri, Grace, 129

Clough, Sheryl, 162, 196

Cook, Nancy L., 43

Corso, Paola, 48

Danon, Ruth, 132, 198

Davison, Thomas, 156

Dawes, Kwame, 51, 52

Dawidoff, Sally, 164

Derricotte, Toi, 54, 56, 134, 136

Dove, Rita, 57

Eady, Cornelius, 58, 59

Farrell, Elizabeth Brulé, 6

Fay, Lisa, 166

Finch, Annie, 199, 200

Fragos, Emily, 7

Franklin, Jennifer, 8, 133

Gale, Kate, 10

Gallagher, Tess, 139, 201

Gay, Ross, 60, 61

Gillan, Maria Mazziotti, 62

Gioseffi, Daniela, 64

Hadas, Rachel, 66, 202

Herrera, Juan Felipe, 63

Hightower, Scott, 69

Hilles, Rick, 204, 206

Hillman, Brenda, 68

Hirshfield, Jane, 72, 138, 208

Hogue, Cynthia, 209

Hostovsky, Paul, 167, 168

Hotchkiss, Melissa, 12

Jackson, Major, 73, 169

Jeffers, Honorée Fannone, 74

Jones, Patricia Spears, 16, 18

Komunyakaa, Yusef, 76, 78

Laskar, Devi S., 79, 84

Limón, Ada, 82

Lisella, Maria, 85, 86

Lowery, Scott, 170, 172

Massimilla, Stephen, xvii, 20, 88, 89, 210

Meinhard, Hermine, 22

Molberg, Jenny, 142, 143. 212

Nezhukumatathi, Aimee, 174

Nye, Naomi Shihab, 92, 176

Oberman, Miller, 146, 178

Paschen, Elise, 93

Peacock, Molly, 13, 14

Rachlin, Ellen, 152, 213

Reevy, Tony, 177

Rekdal, Paisley, 94, 148

Sanchez, Sonia, 96

Schmitt, Peter, 98

Schneider, Jennifer, 181

Sexton, Elaine, 214

Shalforoosh, Soraya, 184, 185

Sharif, Solmaz, 97

Sharma, Yuyutsu, 216

Shiffrin, Nancy, 26

Sideris, Hilary, 100

Stefanescu, Alina, 220, 222

Taylor, Mervyn, 101, 102, 104

Terrone, Maria, 28, 105

Tohe, Laura, 106, 215

Tretheway, Natasha, 108

Wallace, George, 110, 112

Waters, Michael, 224, 225

Wentworth, Marjory, 113

Wheeler, Lesley, 150, 151

Woodard, Catherine, 180

Yahiaoui, Dylan, 185

Young, Kevin, 118

Yvonne, 116

NOTES ON CONTRIBUTORS

Kim Addonizio is the author of a dozen books of poetry and prose. Her most recent poetry collection is *Now We're Getting Somewhere* (W.W. Norton). Her memoir-in-essays, *Bukowski in a Sundress*, was published by Penguin. She has received NEA and Guggenheim Fellowships, as well as Pushcart Prizes in both poetry and the essay. Addonizio's poetry has been widely translated and anthologized. Her work has appeared in the *New Yorker*, the *New York Times*, *Poetry*, *The Sun*, the *Times Literary Supplement* (UK), and numerous literary journals. *Tell Me* was a National Book Award Finalist in poetry. She performs and teaches internationally at colleges, universities, festivals, and conferences; and she currently lives in Oakland, CA, where she teaches private workshops. Website: https://www.kimaddonizio.com

Carol Alexander is the author of the poetry collections *Fever and Bone* (Dos Madres Press, 2021), *Environments* (Dos Madres Press, 2018), and *Habitat Lost* (Cave Moon Press, 2017), as well as the chapbook *Bridal Veil Valls* (Flutter Press, 2013). Her poems have appeared in various anthologies and in journals such as *The American Journal of Poetry*, *The Common*, *Cumberland River Review*, *Denver Quarterly*, *Hamilton Stone Review*, *One*, *Pif*, *The Seattle Review of Books*, *Southern Humanities Review*, *Terrain.org*, and *Third Wednesday*. Alexander holds a PhD in American Literature from Columbia University. A former adjunct lecturer, she is a writer and editor in the field of educational publishing and the author of children's nonfiction.

Elizabeth Alexander—poet, educator, memoirist, scholar, and cultural advocate—is president of The Andrew W. Mellon Foundation, the nation's largest funder in arts, culture, and the humanities in higher education. Dr. Alexander is the author or co-author of fourteen books. Her 2006 poetry book, *American Sublime*, and her 2015 memoir, *The Light of the World*, were both finalists for the Pulitzer Prize. She has held distinguished professorships at Smith College, Columbia University, and Yale University, where she taught for fifteen years and chaired the African American Studies Department. She has served on the Pulitzer Prize Board, and as a Chancellor of the Academy of American Poets, and co-designed the Art for Justice Fund. Alexander composed and delivered "Praise Song for the Day" for the inauguration of President Barack Obama in 2009.

Joel Allegretti is the author of, most recently, *Platypus* (NYQ Books, 2017), a collection of poems, prose, and performance texts, and *Our Dolphin* (Thrice Publishing, 2016), a novella. He is the editor of *Rabbit Ears: TV Poems* (NYQ Books, 2015), which *The Boston Globe* called "cleverly edited" and "a smart exploration of the many, many meanings of TV." Allegretti has published his poems in *The New York Quarterly, Barrow Street, Smartish Pace, PANK,* and many other national journals, as well as in journals published in Canada, the United Kingdom, Belgium, and India. His short stories have appeared in *The MacGuffin, The Adroit Journal,* and *Pennsylvania Literary Journal,* among others. He supplied the texts for three song cycles by the late Frank Ezra Levy, whose recorded work is available in the Naxos American Classics series. Allegretti is a member of the Academy of American Poets and ASCAP.

Desirée Alvarez is a painter and poet whose second book, *Raft of Flame,* was awarded the Omnidawn 2019 Lake Merritt Poetry Book Prize. Her first book of poems, *Devil's Paintbrush,* won the May Sarton New Hampshire Poetry Prize. Her poems have appeared in *Poetry Magazine, Boston Review, Fence,* the *Iowa Review,* and several anthologies. Her work has received an American Academy of Arts and Letters Willard L. Metcalf Award, Artist Fellowships from New York Foundation for the Arts, and a European Capital of Culture Award. She exhibits widely and teaches at City Tech, CUNY, and The Juilliard School.

Hala Alyan is the author of the novel *Salt Houses,* winner of the Dayton Literary Peace Prize and the Arab American Book Award and a finalist for the Chautauqua Prize. She is the author of four award-winning collections of poetry, most recently *The Twenty-Ninth Year.* Her work has been published by *The New Yorker,* the Academy of American Poets, *Lit Hub, The New York Times Book Review, Guernica,* and many other publications. Her novel *The Arsonist's City* is forthcoming. She lives with her husband in Brooklyn, where she works as a clinical psychologist.

Ellen Bass's most recent books are *Indigo* (Copper Canyon, 2020), *Like a Beggar* (Copper Canyon, 2014), and *The Human Line* (Copper Canyon, 2007). She coedited the first major anthology of women's poetry, *No More Masks!* (Doubleday, 1973), and coauthored *The Courage to Heal: A Guide for Women Survivors of Child Sexual Abuse* (HarperCollins, 1988). Among her honors are Fellowships from The Guggenheim Foundation, The National Endowment for the Arts, and the California Arts Council; and awards such as The Lambda Literary Award and three Pushcart Prizes. Bass founded poetry workshops at Salinas Valley State Prison and the Santa Cruz County jails, and teaches in the MFA program in writing at Pacific University. She is currently serving as a Chancellor of the Academy of American Poets.

Reginald Dwayne Betts is a 2021 MacArthur Fellow, a 2018 Guggenheim Fellow and a 2018 NEA Fellow. His writing has generated national attention and earned him a Soros Justice Fellowship, a Radcliffe Fellowship, a Ruth Lilly Fellowship, an NAACP Image Award, and a New America Fellowship. Betts has been featured in *The New York Times*, *The New Yorker*, and the *Washington Post*, and interviewed on NPR's *Fresh Air*, The Travis Smiley Show, and several other national shows. He holds a BA from the University of Maryland; an MFA from Warren Wilson College, where he was a Holden Fellow; and a JD from Yale Law School, where he was awarded the Israel H. Perez Prize for the best student comment in the *Yale Law Journal*. He is a PhD in Law candidate at Yale and, as a Liman Fellow, spent a year representing clients in the New Haven Public Defender's Office.

Jaswinder Bolina is an American poet and writer. His first collection of essays, *Of Color,* was published in June 2020 by McSweeney's Publishing. His most recent collection of poetry, *The 44th of July*, released by Omnidawn in April 2019, was named a finalist for the 2019 Big Other Book Award and was longlisted for the 2019 PEN America Open Book Award. His previous collections include *Phantom Camera* (winner of the 2012 Green Rose Prize in Poetry from New Issues Press), *Carrier Wave* (winner of the 2006 Colorado Prize for Poetry from the Center for Literary Publishing at Colorado State University), and the digital chapbook *The Tallest Building in America* (*Floating Wolf Quarterly*, 2014). An international edition of *Phantom Camera* is available from Hatchette India. His poems have appeared in numerous literary journals and been included in *The Best American Poetry* series.

Rosalind Brenner is a painter, poet, and glass artist who lives and works in eastern Long Island. She is the author of the poetry collection *Every Glittering Chimera* (Blue Light Press), the chapbook *Omega's Garden* (Finishing Line Press), and *All That's Left: Poems and Paintings.* Her poems have appeared in *The Cortland Review, Poetry Bay, The Southampton Review, Long Island Sounds,* Walt's Corner, *Taproot Journal, Performance Poets Literary Review, Ontologica, Tiny Seed Journal,* and *The Arroyo Review,* among other journals, as well as *Broken Circles* (the Cave Moon Press anthology to combat hunger) and the anthologies *Shouts and Whispers* and *From Everywhere a Little.* She received Honorable Mentions in writing contests held by *New Millennium Writings* and *Poetica Magazine: Contemporary Jewish Writing.* She holds an MFA from Sarah Lawrence College.

Lauren Camp is the author of five poetry collections, including *Took House* (Tupelo Press, 2020), a semi-finalist for the North American Book Award. *Turquoise Door* (3: A Taos Press, 2018) was a finalist for the New Mexico-Arizona Book Award. *One Hundred Hungers* (Tupelo Press, 2016) won the Dorset Prize and was a finalist for the Arab American Book Award, the Housatonic Book Award, and the Sheila Margaret Motton Prize. Her poems have appeared in *The Los Angeles Review, Pleiades, Poet Lore, Beloit Poetry Journal,* and *Witness.* An emeritus Black Earth Institute fellow, she has been a visiting scholar at the Mayo Clinic and been awarded residencies at The Taft-Nicholson Center, Storyknife Writers Retreat, and Marble House Project. In 2020, she was selected to be one of 100 international artists for 100 Offerings of Peace. Her poems have been translated into Mandarin, Turkish, Spanish, and Arabic.

Tina Cane serves as the Poet Laureate of Rhode Island, where she is the founder and director of Writers-in-the-Schools, RI. Cane was born and raised in New York City. She is the author of *The Fifth Thought* (Other Painters Press, 2008), *Dear Elena: Letters for Elena Ferrante,* poems with art by Esther Solondz (Skillman Avenue Press, 2016), *Once More with Feeling* (Veliz Books, 2017), and *Body of Work* (Veliz Books, 2019). In 2016, Tina received the Fellowship Merit Award in Poetry from the Rhode Island State Council on the Arts. She is also a 2020 Poet

Laureate Fellow with the Academy of American Poets and the creator/curator of the distance reading series, *Poetry is Bread*. Her new poetry collection, *Year of the Murder Hornet*, is forthcoming from Veliz Books, and her debut novel-in-verse for young adults, *Alma Presses Play*, is forthcoming from Penguin/Random House.

Grace Cavalieri, Maryland's tenth Poet Laureate, is the author of twenty-six books and chapbooks of poetry and several short-form and full-length plays. Her new book of poems is *Grace Art: Poems and Paintings* (Poets' Choice, 2021). Previous publications include *What The Psychic Said* (Goss publications, 2019) and *Showboat* (Goss, 2018), which is about twenty-five years as a Navy wife. Her latest play, "Quilting the Sun," was produced at the Theater for the New City in 2019. She founded and still produces "The Poet and The Poem" for public radio, now from the Library of Congress, celebrating forty-four years on air. Grace holds the AWP's George Garrett Award, the PEN Syndicated Fiction Award, the Allen Ginsberg Award, the Bordighera Poetry Prize, the Paterson Poetry Prize, The Folger Shakespeare Library Columbia Award, and The CPB Silver Medal. Forthcoming books are *The Secret Letters of Madame de Stael* (Goss Publications, 2021) and *New and Selected Poems* (The Word Works, 2022).

Sheryl Clough is a poet, writer, and photographer. She has worked as a paralegal, river guide, editor, Upward Bound teacher, and college instructor. Honors include a nonfiction prize from Jane's Stories, a First Place poetry award from *Third Wednesday*, the William Stafford Award from the Washington Poets Association, and a chapbook prize from the San Gabriel Valley Literary Festival. Her current work in progress is a memoir in poems, featuring friends and family members. She returned to her native Puget Sound after several years in Alaska and now lives on Whidbey Island.

Nancy L. Cook runs "The Witness Project," a program of free community writing workshops in Minneapolis designed to enable creative work by underrepresented voices, and also serves as the flash fiction editor of Kallisto Gaia Press. She has twice been nominated for a Pushcart Prize and has been awarded grants from, among others, the Minnesota State Arts Board, the National Parks Arts Foundation, the Mayo Clinic, and Integrity Arts and Culture. Some of her newest work can be found in *Levitate, Humana Obscura,* and the *Michigan Quarterly Review*.

Paola Corso is the author of seven poetry and fiction books set in her native Pittsburgh, where her Southern Italian immigrant family worked in the steel mills. Her books include *Vertical Bridges: Poems and Photographs of City Steps*; *The Laundress Catches Her Breath,* winner of the Tillie Olsen Award in Creative Writing; *Once I Was Told the Air Was Not for Breathing*, winner of the Triangle Fire Memorial Association Award; and *Catina's Haircut: A Novel in Stories,* a Sons of Italy National Book Club Selection. Her work has appeared in *The New York Times, The Christian Science Monitor, Writer's Digest*, the *Women's Review of Books, US Catholic, The Progressive*, and numerous anthologies. Honors include a New York Foundation for the Arts Poetry Fellowship, a Sherwood Anderson Fiction Prize, inclusion on the Pennsylvania Center for the Book's Cultural Map, and a National Endowment for the Arts WritersCorps Artist Residency.

Ruth Danon is the author of three books of poetry: *Word Has It* (Nirala, 2018), *Limitless Tiny Boat* (BlazeVOX, 2016), and *Triangulation from a Known Point* (North Star Line, 1990). Her work has been published widely in the US and abroad. Robert Creeley selected one of her poems for inclusion in *Best American Poetry 2002*. She lives in Beacon, NY and teaches privately, working with students in Beacon, New York City, and across the country. She teaches for New York Writers Workshop. For twenty-three years she taught creative and expository writing in the program she designed and directed for adult undergraduates at NYU's School of Professional Studies, from which she retired in 2017. She then founded "Live Writing: A Project for the Reading, Writing, and Performance of Poetry" and before the pandemic was the curator of the Spring Street Reading Series for Atlas Studios in Newburgh, New York.

Thomas Davison teaches at two all-male prison facilities in Northern Ohio. He has been deeply moved by his interactions with incarcerated students and has been motivated to create poems and short stories about these experiences. He started the non-profit Entrepreneurial Services for Felons (ESF). This NFP provides free one-on-one support services for felons. Dr. Davison donates a hundred percent of his writing earnings to ESF.

Kwame Dawes, often called "the busiest man in literature," is the author of twenty books of poetry and numerous books of fiction, criticism, and essays;

his most recent poetry collection is *Nebraska* (UNP, 2019). *Speak from Here to There*, a collection of verse co-written with Australian poet John Kinsella, appeared in 2016. The Glenna Luschei Editor of *Prairie Schooner*, Dawes teaches at the University of Nebraska and in the Pacific MFA Program. He is the Director of the African Poetry Book Fund and the Artistic Director of the Calabash International Literary Festival. He has edited several anthologies and is featured frequently on National Public Radio. His awards and honors include the Hollis Summers Prize for Poetry, a Pushcart Prize, the Hurston/Wright Legacy Award, the *Poets and Writers* Barnes and Noble Writers for Writers Award, and a Guggenheim Foundation fellowship. In 2009 he won an Emmy for LiveHopeLove.com, an interactive site based on his Pulitzer Center project, HOPE: Living and Loving with AIDS in Jamaica.

Sally Dawidoff's poetry has appeared in *The Paris Review*, *The Boston Review*, *Ploughshares*, and many other periodicals. She has been awarded fellowships from the National Endowment for the Arts and artists' residencies in the US and abroad, including Centrum in 2021. Her adaptation of Ha Jin's *The Crazed* premiered at Central Works Theater on the twenty-fifth anniversary of the Tiananmen Square Massacre. She and artist Georgia June Goldberg won The Commission with their design for a site-specific multimedia installation of poetry and sculpture. *Pets I've Known,* a song cycle co-written with composer Jason Atkinson, was recorded by guitarist Oren Fader and soprano Eileen Clark. Dawidoff lives in New York City, where she was teaching middle-school English on 9/11.

Toi Derricotte is the author of the National Book Awards Finalist *I: New & Selected Poems* (University of Pittsburgh Press, 2019), *The Undertaker's Daughter* (2011), and four earlier collections, including *Tender*, winner of the 1998 Paterson Poetry Prize. *The Black Notebooks* (W.W. Norton), received the 1998 Anisfield-Wolf Book Award for Non-Fiction and was a *New York Times* Notable Book of the Year. Other honors include the 2012 Paterson Prize for Sustained Literary Achievement and the 2012 PEN/Voelcker Award for Poetry. She won the Lucille Medwick Memorial Award and the 2020 Frost Medal from the Poetry Society of America, as well as three Pushcart Prizes and the Distinguished Pioneering of the Arts Award from the United Black Artists. Professor Emerita at the University of Pittsburgh, Derricotte co-founded Cave Canem and has served on its Board of Directors, as well as on the advisory boards of the Academy of American Poets' Board of Chancellors, 2012–2017, Marsh Hawk Press, and Alice James Books.

Rita Dove is the author of nine collections of poetry, including *Thomas and Beulah* (1986), winner of the Pulitzer Prize; *On the Bus with Rosa Parks* (1999), a *New York Times* Notable Book of the Year; and *Collected Poems 1974–2004*. She is the author of a book of short stories, a novel, and a play, and the editor of two volumes of poetry. Dove has served as Poet Laureate Consultant in Poetry to the Library of Congress, Poet Laureate of the Commonwealth of Virginia from 2004–2006, and a Chancellor of the Academy of American Poets. Other honors include fellowships from the National Endowment for the Arts and the Guggenheim Foundation, the Heinz Award in the Arts and Humanities, the National Humanities Medal, the Fulbright Lifetime Achievement Medal, and the National Medal of Arts. Dove teaches at the University of Virginia, where she is currently the Commonwealth Professor of English.

Cornelius Eady is the author of eight books of poetry, including *Hardheaded Weather: New and Selected Poems* (Putnam, 2002). His second book, *Victims of the Latest Dance Craze*, won the Lamont Prize from the Academy of American Poets in 1985; in 2001 *Brutal Imagination* was a finalist for the National Book Award. His work in theater includes the libretto for the opera "Running Man," a finalist for the Pulitzer Prize in Drama in 1999. His play, "Brutal Imagination," won *Newsday*'s Oppenheimer Award in 2002. In 1996 Eady co-founded, with Toi Derricotte, the Cave Canem summer workshop/retreat for African American poets. More than a decade later, Cave Canem is a thriving national network of black poets, as well as an institution offering regional workshops, readings, and a first book prize. Eady has been a teacher for more than twenty years and is now a professor at Notre Dame University.

Elizabeth Brulé Farrell has been an advertising copy writer in Chicago, a teacher, a tutor, and a writer-in-residence in the public school system. In each setting she has enjoyed encouraging others to express themselves with confidence. Her poems have been published in *The Paterson Literary Review*, *Poetry East*, *The Comstock Review*, *The Healing Muse*, *Spillway*, *The Awakenings Review*, *Earth's*

Daughters, Poem Revised, Except for Love: New England Poets Inspired by Donald Hall, Common Ground Review, Steam Ticket, Pilgrimage, Another Chicago Magazine, The Perch, DailyGood, and more. Forthcoming work will appear in *Evening Street Review.* She has been the recipient of the Louise Bogan Memorial Award for Poetry.

Lisa Fay is a 1978 graduate of Framingham State University with a BA in liberal studies. She also spent a semester abroad at Digby Stuart College, London, England, from 1977 to 1978. Since then, she has had painting and photography exhibitions. However, poetry is her first love. She started writing because cerebral palsy made speech difficult. Fay has published poetry in magazines, newsletters, newspapers, and anthologies. She first achieved recognition with a poem published on the Orange Line in Boston in 1993. One of her poems was displayed at Boston City Hall from September 2018 to April 2019.

Annie Finch is the author of seven books of poetry, including *The Poetry Witch Little Book of Spells, Calendars* (finalist for the National Poetry Series), *Spells: New and Selected Poems,* and the epic poem, *Among the Goddesses: An Epic Libretto in Seven Dreams* (Sarasvati Award from ASWM, 2012). She has also authored *The Body of Poetry: Essays on Women, Form, and the Poetic Self* and *A Poet's Craft: A Comprehensive Guide to Making and Sharing Your Poetry* (University of Michigan Press), as well as the anthologies *A Formal Feeling Comes: Poems in Form by Contemporary Women, Villanelles,* and *Choice Words: Writers on Abortion.* Her work has been published in *Poetry, The Paris Review, The New York Times,* and *The Penguin Book of Twentieth-Century American Poetry.* She holds a BA from Yale and a PhD from Stanford and was awarded the Robert Fitzgerald Award for her lifetime contribution to the study of Versification.

Emily Fragos is a recipient of the Guggenheim Fellowship in Poetry, The Witter Bynner Poetry Prize from the Library of Congress, and the Literature Award from the American Academy of Arts & Letters. She is the author of four books of poetry: *Unrest* (Sheep Meadow, 2021), *Saint Torch, Hostage,* and *Little Savage,* and the editor of seven poetry anthologies for The Everyman's Pocket Library: *Music's Spell, Art & Artists, The Great Cat, The Dance, The Letters of Emily Dickinson, Poems of Gratitude,* and *Poems of Paris.* She has also written numerous articles on music and dance and served as guest poetry editor for *Guernica*. Emily Fragos has taught at Columbia University, Yale, and NYU. She lives in New York City.

Jennifer Franklin is the author of two full-length collections, most recently *No Small Gift* (Four Way Books, 2018). Her third book, *If Some God Shakes Your House*, will be published by Four Way Books in 2023. Her work has been published or is forthcoming in *American Poetry Review, Blackbird, Boston Review, Broadsided Press, Gettysburg Review, Guernica, JAMA, Los Angeles Review, Love's Executive Order, The Nation, New England Review, Paris Review, Plume*, Poem-a-Day on poets.org, and *Prairie Schooner*. She holds an AB from Brown University and an MFA from Columbia University, where she was the Harvey Baker Fellow. For the past seven years, she has taught manuscript revision at the Hudson Valley Writer's Center, where she runs the reading series, serves as Program Director, and is a co-editor at Slapering Hol Press. She lives in New York City.

Kate Gale is co-founder and Managing Editor of Red Hen Press and Editor of the *Los Angeles Review*. She teaches in the Low Residency MFA program at the University of Nebraska in Poetry, Fiction, and Creative Non-Fiction. She is the author of the forthcoming *The Loneliest Girl* from the University of New Mexico Press and seven books of poetry, including *The Goldilocks Zone* from the University of New Mexico Press (2014) and *Echo Light* from Red Mountain (2014), as well as six librettos, including *Rio de Sangre*, with composer Don Davis, which had its world premiere in October 2010 at the Florentine Opera in Milwaukee. Dr. Gale speaks on independent publishing around the US at colleges and universities such as USC and Columbia, and at Oxford. Her opera on Che Guevara (at https://www.thewebopera.com/) is in process in collaboration with Cuban composer Armando Bayolo.

Tess Gallagher is a poet, essayist, novelist, and playwright. She received a BA and an MA from the University of Washington and an MFA from the University of Iowa. Her first collection, *Instructions to the Double*, won the 1976 Elliston Book Award for "the best book of poetry published by a small press." In 1984 she published the collection *Willingly*, poems written to and about her third husband, author Raymond Carver. Other collections include *Dear Ghosts* (Graywolf Press,

2006), *My Black Horse: New and Selected Poems* (1995), *Owl-Spirit Dwelling* (1994), and *Moon Crossing Bridge* (1992). Her honors include a fellowship from the Guggenheim Foundation, two National Endowment of the Arts Awards, and the Maxine Cushing Gray Foundation Award. Gallagher has taught at St. Lawrence University, Kirkland College, the University of Montana in Missoula, the University of Arizona in Tucson, Syracuse University, Willamette University, Bucknell University, and Whitman College.

Ross Gay is the author of four books of poetry: *Against Which, Bringing the Shovel Down, Be Holding,* and *Catalog of Unabashed Gratitude,* winner of the 2015 National Book Critics Circle Award and the 2016 Kingsley Tufts Poetry Award. His collection of essays, *The Book of Delights,* was released by Algonquin Books in 2019. Ross is also co-author, with Aimee Nezhukumatathil, of the chapbook "Lace and Pyrite: Letters from Two Gardens," and co-author, with Rosechard Wehrenberg, of the chapbook, "River." He is a founding editor, with Karissa Chen and Patrick Rosal, of the online sports magazine *Some Call it Ballin'.* Ross is also an editor with the chapbook presses Q Avenue and Ledge Mule Press. He has received fellowships from Cave Canem, the Bread Loaf Writer's Conference, and the Guggenheim Foundation. Ross teaches at Indiana University.

Maria Mazziotti Gillan, American Book Award recipient for *All That Lies Between Us* (Guernica Editions) and author of twenty-four books, founded the Poetry Center in Paterson, NJ, is editor of the *Paterson Literary Review* and Professor Emerita of English and creative writing at Binghamton University, SUNY. Her newest poetry collection is *When the Stars Were Still Visible* (Stephen F. Austin University Press, 2021). Other recent publications include *What Blooms in Winter* (NYQ, 2016) and the poetry and photography collaboration with Mark Hillringhouse, *Paterson Light and Shadow* (Serving House Books, 2017). Gillan has read her poems at universities, festivals, and poetry centers throughout the US and in Italy, France, Finland, Wales, and Ireland. Her papers are housed at the Binghamton University Libraries.

Daniela Gioseffi is an American Book Award winning author of eighteen books of poetry and prose. She has won grant awards in poetry from the NY State

Council for the Arts and The John Ciardi Award for Lifetime Achievement in Poetry. She has read her work in many venues and on air for NPR and the BBC. Her latest book of poems is *Waging Beauty as the Polar Bear Dreams of Ice*. Gioseffi has served as editor of the anthology *www.Eco-Poetry.org*. Her papers and books are archived at Yale University's Beinecke Library; her life in writing, social justice and multicultural pioneering is portrayed in a documentary by prize-winning filmmaker Anton Evangelista, *Author and Activist* (*www.AuthorandActivist.com*), which premiered at The Maya Deren Theatre, Manhattan in 2014 and has been screened on campuses throughout the Northeast. For more information: *www.DanielaGioseffi.com*. Her work is published online at the Poetry Foundation of America and the Academy of American Poets.

Rachel Hadas is the author of many books of poetry, essays, and translations, including the prose work *Piece by Piece* (Paul Dry Books) and the poetry collection *Love and Dread* (Measure Press). Hadas's honors include a Guggenheim Fellowship, an American Academy of Arts and Letters Award in Literature, the O.B. Hardison Prize, and a fellowship at the Cullman Center for Scholars and Writers at the New York Public Library. She has translated tragedies by Euripides (*The Two Iphigenia Plays*, Northwestern University Press, 2018), and, most recently, one book of Nonnus's long epic *The Dionysiaca*, forthcoming in 2022 from the University of Michigan Press. Rachel Hadas is Board of Governors Professor of English at Rutgers University-Newark, where she has taught for many years.

Scott Hightower is the author of four books of poetry published in the US and two bilingual (English/Spanish) collections in Madrid. Hightower is also the editor of the bilingual anthology *Women Rowing: Mujeres a los remos* (Mantis Editores). His translations of Spanish poetry garnered a Willis Barnstone Translation Prize, and his *Part of the Bargain* received Copper Canyon Press's Hayden Carruth Award. His poems have appeared in the *Yale Review*, *Salmagundi*, *Ploughshares*, *AGNI*, *New England Review*, *Gulf Coast*, and elsewhere. He lives in Manhattan, sojourns in Spain, and currently teaches at New York University's Gallatin School of Individualized Study.

Rick Hilles is the author of the poetry collections *Brother Salvage*, winner of the

2005 Agnes Lynch Starrett Poetry Prize and the 2006 Foreword Poetry Book of the Year, and *A Map of the Lost World*, a finalist for the Ohioana Book Award. He has been the recipient of a Whiting Award, the Amy Lowell Poetry Traveling Scholarship, a Fulbright, and a Camargo Fellowship. His latest collection is *The Empathy Machine*. He has recent work in *American Literary Review*, *Five Points*, *Kenyon Review*, *Literary Imagination*, *New Letters*, *Ploughshares*, *Plume*, and *The Southern Review*. He teaches in the English Department and MFA Program of Vanderbilt University.

Brenda Hillman is the author of ten collections of poetry: *White Dress*; *Fortress*; *Death Tractates*; *Bright Existence*; *Loose Sugar*; *Cascadia*; *Pieces of Air in the Epic*; *Practical Water* (LA Times Book Award for Poetry); *Seasonal Works with Letters on Fire* (the 2014 Griffin Poetry Prize and the Northern California Book Award for Poetry); and the recent *Extra Hidden Life, among the Days*. In 2016 she was named a Chancellor of the Academy of American Poets. Among other awards Hillman has received are the 2012 Academy of American Poets Fellowship, the 2005 William Carlos Williams Prize for poetry, and Fellowships from the National Endowment for the Arts and the Guggenheim Foundation.

Jane Hirshfield is the author of nine books of poetry, including *Ledger*; *The Beauty*; *Come, Thief*; and *Given Sugar, Given Salt*; and two collections of essays, *Nine Gates: Entering the Mind of Poetry* and *Ten Windows: How Great Poets Transform the World*. She has edited and co-translated four books presenting the work of world poets. Her books have received the Poetry Center Book Award and the California Book Award, and have been finalists for the National Book Critics Circle Award, longlisted for the National Book Award, and shortlisted for England's T.S. Eliot Prize. Hirshfield has received fellowships from the Guggenheim and Rockefeller foundations, the NEA, and the Academy of American Poets, where she has been a Chancellor, and is an inducted member of the American Academy of Arts and Sciences. Her poems appear in *The New Yorker*, *The Atlantic*, *The New York Review of Books*, *The New York Times*, *The Times Literary Supplement*, *Harper's*, *Poetry*, and ten editions of *The Best American Poetry*.

Cynthia Hogue's most recent collections are *Revenance*, listed as one of the 2014 Standout Books by the Academy of American Poets, and *In June the Labyrinth*

(2017). Her tenth collection, *instead, it is dark*, which includes "The Bite of the Apple," will be out from Red Hen Press in 2023. Her translations with Sylvain Gallais include *Fortino Sámano (The overflowing of the poem)*, from the French of Virginie Lalucq and Jean-Luc Nancy, which won the Landon Translation Award from the Academy of American Poets in 2013, and Nicole Brossard's *Lointaines* (forthcoming, 2022). Hogue's forthcoming chapbook is entitled *Contain* (Tram Editions, 2022). Her honors include two NEA Fellowships, a MacDowell Colony residency, a Witter Bynner Translation Fellowship, and the H.D. Fellowship at Yale University. She is the inaugural Marshall Chair in Poetry Emerita Professor of English at Arizona State University and lives in Tucson.

Paul Hostovsky is the author of ten books of poetry and five poetry chapbooks. His poems have been featured on *Poetry Daily*, *Verse Daily*, and *The Writer's Almanac*. He has been published in *Poetry*, *Passages North*, *Carolina Quarterly*, *Shenandoah*, *New Delta Review*, *Bellevue Literary Review*, *Atlanta Review*, *Poetry East*, *The Sun*, and many other journals and anthologies. He has won a Pushcart Prize, the *Comstock Review*'s Muriel Craft Bailey Award, the FutureCycle Poetry Book Prize, and chapbook contests from Grayson Books, Riverstone Press, Frank Cat Press, Split Oak Press, and Sport Literate. He makes his living in Boston as a sign language interpreter. Website: paulhostovsky.com

Melissa Hotchkiss is a poet and editor who lives in Jersey City, NJ. Melissa ran the *Barrow Street* Reading Series for its eight years of existence (1994–2002), has been an editor of the journal *Barrow Street* since it was established in 1998, and is a trustee of Barrow Street, Inc. Melissa's first book of poems, *Storm Damage*, was published by Tupelo Press. Her poems and prose have appeared in numerous publications such as *The American Poetry Review*, *The New York Times*, *Free Inquiry*, *Women's Studies Quarterly*, *Interim*, *Nine Mile*, *trampest*, *Poets for Palestine* (anthology), and others.

Major Jackson is the author of five books of poetry, including *The Absurd Man* (2020), *Roll Deep* (2015), *Holding Company* (2010), *Hoops* (2006), and *Leaving Saturn* (2002), which won the Cave Canem Poetry Prize for a first book of poems. His edited volumes include *Best American Poetry 2019*, *Renga for Obama*, and Library of America's *Countee Cullen: Collected Poems*. A recipient of fellowships from the Fine Arts Work Center in Provincetown, The Guggenheim Foundation, National Endowment for the Arts, and the Radcliffe Institute for Advanced Study at Harvard University, he has also been awarded a Pushcart Prize, a Whiting Writers' Award, and a Pew Fellowship in the Arts and the Witter Bynner Foundation in conjunction with the Library of Congress. His work appears in *American Poetry Review*, *The New Yorker*, *Paris Review*, *Ploughshares*, *Poetry*, and *Poetry London*. Jackson is the Gertrude Conaway Vanderbilt Chair in the Humanities at Vanderbilt University. He serves as the Poetry Editor of *The Harvard Review*.

Honorée Fanonne Jeffers is the author of four critically acclaimed books of poetry: *The Gospel of Barbecue* (Kent State, 2000), *Outlandish Blues* (Wesleyan, 2003), *Red Clay Suite* (Southern Illinois, 2007), and *The Glory Gets* (Wesleyan, 2015). Her poems have appeared in such journals as *American Poetry Review*, *Gettysburg Review*, *Iowa Review*, *Prairie Schooner*, and *Angles of Ascent: A Norton Anthology of Contemporary African American Poetry*. She has been awarded fellowships from the American Antiquarian Society, the Bread Loaf Writers Conference, the National Endowment for the Arts, the Rona Jaffe Foundation, the Vermont Studio Center, and the Witter Bynner Foundation through the Library of Congress. She won the 2018 Harper Lee Award for Literary Distinction, a lifetime achievement award. Her prose writing has also been widely published.

Patricia Spears Jones is the author of the poetry collections *Pain Killer* and *Femme du Monde* (Tia Chucha Press), *The Weather That Kills* (Coffee House Press), and *A Lucent Fire: New and Selected Poems* (White Pine Press), as well as five poetry chapbooks. Her work has been widely anthologized. She is the eleventh winner of The Jackson Poetry Prize, and has been awarded grants from the NEA, the NYFA, and the Barbara Deming Memorial Fund. She has been a fellow at the Virginia Center for Creative Arts, Yaddo, and the Millay Colony. Residencies include the Rauschenberg Residency and The Bau Institute at Camargo Foundation. A contributing editor at *BOMB* magazine, Spears Jones has also served as a program coordinator for the Poetry Project at St. Mark's Church and led the New Works Program for the Massachusetts Council of Arts and Humanities.

Yusef Komunyakaa's most recent books are *The Emperor of Water Clocks* (Farrar, Straus and Giroux, 2015) and *The Chameleon Couch* (FSG, 2011). Other books include *Warhorses* (FSG, 2008); *Taboo: The Wishbone Trilogy, Part 1* (FSG, 2006); *Pleasure Dome: New & Collected Poems, 1975–1999* (Wesleyan University Press, 2001); *Talking Dirty to the Gods* (FSG, 2000). *Thieves of Paradise* (Wesleyan University Press, 1998), a finalist for the National Book Critics Circle Award; and *Magic City* (Wesleyan University Press, 1992). His collection *Neon Vernacular: New & Selected Poems 1977–1989* (Wesleyan University Press, 1994) won the Pulitzer Prize and the Kingsley Tufts Poetry Award. Komunyakaa's prose is collected in *Blue Notes: Interviews and Commentaries* (University of Michigan Press, 2000). He co-edited *The Jazz Poetry Anthology*, co-translated *The Insomnia of Fire* by Nguyen Quang Thieu, and served as guest editor for *The Best American Poetry 2003*.

Devi S. Laskar is a poet, photographer, and the author of *The Atlas of Reds and Blues*, winner of 7th annual Crook's Corner Book Prize (2020) for best debut novel set in the South, and winner of the 2020 Asian/Pacific American Award for Literature. The novel was named by *The Washington Post* as one of the 50 best books of 2019. Laskar's poetry and essays have appeared in such publications as *USA Today*, *Rattle*, *Tin House*, and *Evergreen Review*. Finishing Line Press published two poetry chapbooks, *Gas & Food, No Lodging* and *Anastasia Maps*, in 2017; her second novel, *CIRCA*, is forthcoming from Houghton Mifflin Harcourt in spring 2022. A native of Chapel Hill, NC, Laskar now lives in California with her family.

Ada Limón, a Guggenheim fellow, is the author of five poetry collections, including *The Carrying* (Milkweed Editions, 2018), which won the National Book Critics Circle Award for Poetry. Other books include *Bright Dead Things* (Milkweed Editions, 2015), a finalist for the National Book Critics Circle Award; *Lucky Wreck*, a first book that won the 2005 Autumn House Poetry Prize; and *This Big Fake World*, the winner of the Pearl Poetry Prize in 2006. A 2001–2002 fellow at the Provincetown Fine Arts Work Center, she also received a grant from the New York Foundation for the Arts and won the Chicago Literary Award for Poetry. Her work has appeared in numerous publications, including the *New Yorker*, *Harvard Review*, *Pleiades*, and *Barrow Street*. She serves on the faculty of the Queens University of Charlotte Low Residency MFA program and lives in Lexington, Kentucky.

Maria Lisella is the author of three books of poetry, including *Thieves in the Family* (NYQ Books, 2014) and the chapbooks *Amore on Hope Street* (Finishing Line Press, 2009) and *Two Naked Feet* (Poets Wear Prada, 2009). She curates the Italian American Writers Association literary series and is a charter member of the online poetry circle, Brevitas. An award-winning travel writer, her work appears in *USA TODAY*, *The Jerusalem Post*, *Travel Market Report*, and the bilingual *La Voce di New York*. Cited for Honorable Mention for the Allen Ginsberg Poetry Award, Lisella has taught English as a second language and composition at Touro College and has taught Tourism and Hospitality at the Borough of Manhattan Community College. She is the outgoing Poet Laureate of Queens, New York.

Scott Lowery is the author of the chapbook *Empty-handed*, winner of the 2013 Emergence Chapbook Prize from Red Dragonfly Press. His poems have appeared in *Great River Review*, *Naugatuck River Review*, *North American Review*, *Prairie Schooner*, *Sow's Ear Poetry*, *The Teacher's Voice*, *Third Wednesday*, and *Water-Stone Review*. Lowery has been a Pushcart Prize nominee and a finalist for several national poetry prizes. His career as a schoolteacher spanned thirty years in a variety of public settings, including corrections, residential treatment, and alternative programs. After retirement, he has continued working with children as a teaching artist, including through coordination of The Teen Voices Project, a series of writing workshops that resulted in the publication of *Soundings* (Book Shelf Editions). Lowery currently splits his time between Rollingstone, MN, and the Milwaukee area.

Stephen Massimilla is a poet, scholar, professor, and painter. His newest collection, *Frank Dark* (Barrow Street, 2022), is forthcoming. Dr. Massimilla's multi-genre *Cooking with the Muse* (Tupelo Press, 2016) won the Eric Hoffer Award, the National Indie Excellence Award, the Living Now Award, the IAN Book of the Year Award, and many others. Previous books and awards include *The Plague Doctor in His Hull-Shaped Hat* (SFA Press Prize); *Forty Floors from Yesterday* (Bordighera Poetry Prize, CUNY); *Aiaia* (Grolier Poetry Prize); *Second Thought* (Salmon Run National Poetry Book Award runner-up, selected by X.J. Kennedy); the Van Rensselaer Prize, selected by Kenneth Koch; many Pushcart Prize nominations; a study of myth in poetry; and translations of books by Neruda and others. His work has been reviewed widely in publications ranging from *Booklist* to *The Chicago Tribune* to *Huffpost*. He has recent poems in *AGNI*, *American Literary Review*, *Barrow Street*, *Chelsea*, *Colorado Review*, *Denver Quarterly*, *Gulf Coast*, *The Literary Review*, *Poetry Daily*, *Poet Lore*, *The Southern Review*, *Tampa Review*, *Verse Daily*, and hundreds of other journals and anthologies. He holds an MFA and a PhD from Columbia University and teaches at Columbia University and The New School. Websites: www.stephenmassimilla.com and www.cookingwiththemuse.com

Jenny Molberg is the author of *Marvels of the Invisible* (winner of the Berkshire Prize, Tupelo Press, 2017) and *Refusal: Poems* (LSU Press, 2020). She coedited the Unsung Masters Series collection *Adelaide Crapsey: On the Life & Work of an American Master*. Her poems have appeared or are forthcoming in *Ploughshares*, *Gulf Coast*, *The Missouri Review*, *Poetry International*, *Boulevard*, *Copper Nickel*, *The Adroit Journal*, *Best New Poets*, and other publications. She is the recipient of a 2019–2020 Creative Writing Fellowship from the National Endowment for the Arts, as well as scholarships and fellowships from the Sewanee Writers Conference, the C.D. Wright Conference, the Longleaf Writers Conference, and the Vermont Studio Center. Molberg holds a BA from Louisiana State University, an MFA from American University, and a PhD from the University of North Texas. She is Associate Professor of Creative Writing at the University of Central Missouri, where she directs Pleiades Press and edits *Pleiades: Literature in Context*.

Hermine Meinhard's book *Bright Turquoise Umbrella,* published by Tupelo Press, was a finalist for the Poetry Society of America's Norma Farber First Book Award. Her poems have appeared in *American Letters & Commentary, Barrow Street, Drunken Boat, Verse Daily, How2,* and many other publications. Meinhard conceived, curates and hosts *Nights of the Fireflies,* a reading series presented by the JCC Manhattan via Zoom. Since the mid-90s she has performed her work throughout New York City, the East Coast and the Midwest at such venues as Live from Prairie Lights Book Store, The Kitchen, Cornelia Street Cafe, KGB Bar, the Bowery Poetry Club, and Hudson Valley Writers Center, to name a few. A founding member of New York Writers Workshop, she teaches at the

Marlene Meyerson JCC Manhattan and is a professor of writing in the School of Professional Studies at NYU. Meinhard's playful, improvisational teaching methods help her students to write intuitively and bring the depth and vitality of their lives to their work.

Aimee Nezhukumatathil is the author of the *New York Times* best-selling illustrated collection of nature essays and Kirkus Prize finalist, *World of Wonders: In Praise of Fireflies, Whale Sharks, & Other Astonishments* (Milkweed Editions, 2020), Barnes and Noble's Book of the Year. Her four previous poetry collections are *Oceanic* (Copper Canyon Press, 2018), *Lucky Fish* (2011), *At the Drive-in Volcano* (2007), and *Miracle Fruit* (2003), the last three from Tupelo Press. Her most recent chapbook is *Lace and Pyrite*, a collaboration of garden poems with poet Ross Gay. Her writing appears in the *Best American Poetry Series, The New York Times Magazine, ESPN, Ploughshares, American Poetry Review*, and *Tin House*. Honors include a poetry fellowship from the National Endowment for the Arts, a Pushcart Prize, and a Mississippi Arts Council grant. She has also been named a Guggenheim Fellow in poetry. She is Professor of English and Creative Writing in the University of Mississippi's MFA program.

Naomi Shihab Nye is the author of numerous books of poems, most recently *Cast Away: Poems for Our Time* (Greenwillow Books, 2020). Her other books of poetry include *The Tiny Journalist* (BOA Editions, 2019); *Voices in the Air: Poems for Listeners* (Greenwillow Books, 2018); *Transfer* (BOA Editions, 2011); *You and Yours* (BOA Editions, 2005), which received the Isabella Gardner Poetry Award; and *19 Varieties of Gazelle: Poems of the Middle East* (Greenwillow Books, 2002), a collection of new and selected poems about the Middle East. She is also the author of several books of poetry and fiction for children, including *Habibi* (Simon Pulse, 1997), for which she received the Jane Addams Children's Book award in 1998. Other awards include the Ivan Sandrof Award for Lifetime Achievement from the National Book Critics Circle, the Lavan Award, the Paterson Poetry Prize, the Carity Randall Prize, and many Pushcart Prizes.

Miller Oberman is the author of *The Unstill Ones,* poems and translations, published as part of the Princeton Series of Contemporary Poets, 2017. He has received a number of awards for his poetry, including a Ruth Lilly Fellowship, a

92Y Discovery Prize, and *Poetry* magazine's John Frederick Nims Memorial Prize for Translation. Poems from *The Unstill Ones* appeared in *Poetry*, *London Review of Books*, *The Nation*, *Boston Review*, *Tin House*, and *Harvard Review*. Poems from his current project, "Joshua," have appeared or are forthcoming in *The New Yorker*, *Poetry*, Poem-a-Day, and *Foglifter*. Miller is an editor at Broadsided Press, which publishes monthly visual-literary collaborations as free posters for anyone to download and print. He teaches poetry workshops at Brooklyn Poets, and teaches in and directs the First-Year Writing program at Eugene Lang College of The New School.

Elise Paschen is the author of *The Nightlife*, *Bestiary*, *Infidelities* (winner of the Nicholas Roerich Poetry Prize), and *Houses: Coasts*. Her poems have appeared in *A Norton Anthology of Native Nations Poetry*, *Best American Poetry*, *The New Yorker*, and *Poetry*, among other anthologies and magazines. She has edited many anthologies, including *The Eloquent Poem*, as well as *The New York Times* best-selling *Poetry Speaks*. An enrolled member of the Osage Nation, Paschen is a recipient of the Rupert Costo Chair in American Indian Affairs Medal. Former Executive Director of the Poetry Society of America, she is a co-founder of Poetry in Motion, a nationwide program which places poetry posters in subway cars and buses. Dr. Paschen teaches in the MFA Writing Program at the School of the Art Institute of Chicago.

Molly Peacock is the author of seven books of poetry, including *The Analyst: Poems* and *Cornucopia: New and Selected Poems*. Her work appears in leading literary journals such as *Poetry* and *Plume* and is anthologized in *The Oxford Book of American Poetry*. Peacock was co-creator of Poetry in Motion on New York City's subways and buses and inaugurated The Best Canadian Poetry series. She is the author of the biographies *The Paper Garden: Mrs. Delany Begins Her Life's Work at 72* and *Flower Diary: Mary Hiester Reid Paints, Travels, Marries & Opens a Door*. She teaches at the Unterberg Poetry Center of New York's 92Y and sponsors The Secret Poetry Room at Binghamton University. A dual Canadian and US citizen, she lives in Toronto.

Ellen Rachlin's poetry collections include *Until Crazy Catches Me* (Antrim House, 2008) and *Permeable Divide* (Antrim House, 2017), a 2018 IBPA

Benjamin Franklin Silver Award recipient and finalist for the 2018 Best Book Award. She is the author of two chapbooks, *Waiting for Here* (Finishing Line Press, 2004), a finalist for the New Women's Voices series and *Captive to Residue* (Flarestack Publishing, UK, 2009). Her poems have appeared in various journals, anthologies, and books, including *American Poetry Review, Comstock Review, Granta, Literary Imagination, Court Green, The Eloquent Poem,* and *The Good Grief Journal.* She holds an MFA from Antioch University, serves as Treasurer of The Poetry Society of America and on the boards of other nonprofits, spent her career in finance, and is a Grand Master in taekwondo and a lifelong dance student.

Tony Reevy is the author of the poetry chapbooks *Green Cove Stop, Magdalena, Lightning in Wartime,* and *In Mountain Lion Country,* and the poetry collections *Old North, Passage* and *Socorro.* His fiction and non-fiction books include *Ghost Train!, O. Winston Link: Life Along the Line, The Railroad Photography of Jack Delano* and *The Railroad Photography of Lucius Beebe and Charles Clegg.* He resides in Durham, North Carolina.

Paisley Rekdal is the author of five books of poetry: *A Crash of Rhinos, Six Girls Without Pants, The Invention of the Kaleidoscope, Animal Eye,* and *Imaginary Vessels.* Her work has received a Guggenheim Fellowship, the Amy Lowell Poetry Traveling Fellowship, a Village Voice Writers on the Verge Award, an NEA Fellowship, Pushcart Prizes, the University of Georgia Press' Contemporary Poetry Series Award, a Fulbright Fellowship, the AWP Creative Nonfiction Award, inclusion in the *Best American Poetry* series, and various state arts council awards. Her poems and essays have appeared in *The New York Times Magazine, American Poetry Review, The Kenyon Review, Poetry, The New Republic, Virginia Quarterly Review,* and *Tin House,* and on National Public Radio. Her latest collection, *Nightingale,* was published in 2019. Rekdal's book on cultural appropriation, *Appropriate: A Provocation,* was published by W.W. Norton in 2021. She was the *Best American Poetry Series* guest editor for 2020. In May 2017, Paisley was named Utah's Poet Laureate.

Sonia Sanchez is the author of more than a dozen books of poetry, including *Morning Haiku* (Beacon Press, 2010); *Shake Loose My Skin: New and Selected*

Poems (Beacon Press, 1999); *Does your house have lions?* (Beacon Press, 1995), nominated for both the NAACP Image Award and the National Book Critics Circle Award; *Homegirls & Handgrenades* (White Pine Press, 1984), which won an American Book Award from the Before Columbus Foundation; *I've Been a Woman: New and Selected Poems* (Third World Press, 1978); *A Blues Book for Blue Black Magical Women* (Broadside Press, 1973); *Love Poems* (Third Press, 1973); *We a BadDDD People* (Broadside Press, 1970); and *Homecoming* (Broadside Press, 1969). Her published plays are *Black Cats Back and Uneasy Landings* (1995), *I'm Black When I'm Singing, I'm Blue When I Ain't* (1982), *Malcolm Man/Don't Live Here No Mo'* (1979), *Uh Huh: But How Do It Free Us?* (1974), *Dirty Hearts 72* (1973), *The Bronx Is Next* (1970), and *Sister Son/ji* (1969).

Peter Schmitt is the author of six collections of poems, including *Goodbye, Apostrophe* (Regal House, 2020). His work is widely published and has received The Discovery/*The Nation* Prize, The Lavan Award from The Academy of American Poets, and the Julia Peterkin Prize, among other honors. His poems have appeared in such journals as *The Hudson Review, The Nation, The Paris Review, Poetry,* and *The Southern Review*. His work has been featured on the Writers Almanac and in numerous anthologies and textbooks. He has taught creative writing and literature at the University of Miami since 1986.

Jennifer Schneider is an educator, attorney, and writer. She lives, writes, and works in small spaces throughout Philadelphia. Recent work appears in *The Popular Culture Studies Journal, Toho Journal, The New Verse News, Zingara Poetry Review, Streetlight Magazine, Chaleur Magazine, LSE Review of Books,* and other literary and scholarly journals.

Elaine Sexton is a poet, critic, teacher, and maker. Her fourth collection of poems, *Drive,* is forthcoming from Grid Books, based in Beacon, NY. She teaches at the Writing Institute at Sarah Lawrence College and has also been a guest faculty member at numerous writing and art programs in the US and abroad, including New York University, City College, and Arts Workshop International. She is an avid bookmaker and micro-publisher of 'zines and chapbooks. Visit her at elainesexton.org.

Soraya Shalforoosh is the author of the poetry collection *This Version of Earth* (Barrow Street, 2014). She has been a featured poet in the Journal of the Academy of American Poets Emerging Poet Series, and has had poems and reviews in *Black Earth Institute, Apogee Journal, Taos Journal, Barrow Street, Lumina Journal, Skanky Possum, Marlboro Review, WSQ, Brink: An Anthology of Postmodern American Poetry,* and *Tribes*.org. Shalforoosh holds an MFA in Creative Writing from The New School and, as an undergraduate at Clark University, won first place in the Prentiss Cheney Hoyt Poetry Contest. She has been a guest poet at William Paterson University in New Jersey, Berkeley College in New York, and San José State University and a guest speaker at the American Embassy in Algeria. Shalforoosh was a poetry fellow at the Frost Place in July 2017.

Solmaz Sharif holds degrees from New York University and the University of California, Berkeley, where she studied and taught in accordance with June Jordan's Poetry for the People program. Her first poetry collection, *LOOK* (Graywolf Press, 2016), was a finalist for the National Book Award in poetry. Her work has appeared in *Poetry, Kenyon Review, jubilat, Gulf Coast, Boston Review, Witness,* and other publications. She is the recipient of fellowships from the Poetry Foundation, the National Endowment for the Arts, and the Rona Jaffe Foundation. Sharif is currently an assistant professor at Arizona State University.

Yuyutsu Sharma is a world-renowned Himalayan poet and translator, recipient of fellowships and grants from The Rockefeller Foundation; the Ireland Literature Exchange; the Trubar Foundation, Slovenia; The Institute for the Translation of Hebrew Literature; and The Foundation for the Production and Translation of Dutch Literature. He has published ten poetry collections, including *The Second Buddha Walk*; *A Blizzard in My Bones: New York Poems*; *Quaking Cantos: Nepal Earthquake Poems*; *Nepal Trilogy*; *Space Cake*; *Amsterdam*; and *Annapurna Poems*. Three of his poetry books, *Poèmes de l' Himalayas, Poemas de Los Himalayas,* and *Jezero Fewa & Konj,* have appeared in French, Spanish and Slovenian respectively. For half of the year, he travels and reads all over the world and conducts creative writing workshops at various universities in North America and Europe; but he goes trekking in the Himalayas when back home. Currently, Yuyutsu Sharma edits *Pratik: A Quarterly Magazine of Contemporary Writing.*

Nancy Shiffrin is the author of three collections of poetry: *The Vast Unknowing* (Infinity Publishing, 2012), *Game with Variations*, and *Flight* (wordpoetrybooks. com). Her work has been published in *The Los Angeles Times, Human Behavior, Shofar, New York Magazine, New York Quarterly, Humanistic Judaism, Lummox Journal, poetix.net*, and numerous other periodicals. Her work has won awards and honorable mentions from the Academy of American Poets, The Alice Jackson Foundation, The Poetry Society of America, The Pushcart Foundation, and the Dora Teitelbaum Foundation.

Hilary Sideris is the author of six poetry chapbooks: *The Orange Juice Is Over* (Finishing Line Press, 2008), *Baby* (Pudding House Press, 2009), *Gold & Other Fish* (Finishing Line Press, 2011), *Sweet Flag* (Finishing Line Press, 2013), and *The Silent B* (Dos Madres Press, 2019), as well as four full-length collections: *Most Likely to Die* (Poets Wear Prada Press, 2014), *The Inclination to Make Waves* (Big Wonderful Press, 2016), *Un Amore Veloce* (Kelsay Books, 2019), and *Animals in English, Poems after Temple Grandin* (Dos Madres Press, 2020). Sideris received her MFA from The University of Iowa Writers' Workshop. Her poems have appeared in *The American Journal of Poetry, Arts & Letters, Barrow Street, The Cortland Review, Connecticut Review, Fourteen Hills, Green Mountains Review, Gulf Coast, Poet Lore, Poetry Daily, Rhino, Quiddity, Salamander, The Southern Poetry Review, Southampton Review, Sugar House Review*, and *Tar River Poetry*. She works as a professional developer for the CUNY Start Program.

Alina Stefanescu is the author of the poetry collection *Stories to Read Aloud to Your Fetus* (Finishing Line Press, 2017) and the chapbooks *pokimen* (Anchor & Plume, 2016), *Letters to Arthur* (Beard of Bees, 2016), and *Objects In Vases* (Anchor & Plume, 2016). Her work has appeared in *Avatar Review, Cider Press Review, Forage, Lunch Ticket*, and *Red Hill Poetry Journal*, among other journals; her fiction has also been widely published. She won the 2016 Alabama State Poetry Society Book of the Year Award and has been a finalist for the Robert Dana Poetry Prize and the Black Warrior Poetry Prize. She serves as Poetry Editor for *Pidgeonholes* and *Random Sample Review*, book reviewer for *Up the Staircase Quarterly* and *GASH*, President Emerita of Alabama State Poetry Society, board member for the Alabama Writer's Cooperative, co-director of PEN America's Birmingham Chapter, and co-founder of 100,000 Poets for Change Birmingham.

Mervyn Taylor, a Trinidad-born poet and longtime Brooklyn resident, has taught at Bronx Community College, The New School, and in the New York City public school system. He is the author of seven books of poetry, including *No Back Door* (2010), *The Waving Gallery* (2014), and most recently, *Country of Warm Snow* (2020), which received a Poetry Book Society Recommendation and was longlisted for the Bocas Poetry Prize. About his work, Derek Walcott said, "Taylor's poems possess an admirable degree of subtlety, and a tone that keeps him separate and unique." A chapbook of poems titled *News of the Living: Corona Poems* was also published in 2020. Currently, he serves as co-editor of Slapering Hol Press, Hudson Valley, NY.

Maria Terrone is the author of the poetry collections *Eye to Eye* (Bordighera Press, 2014), *A Secret Room in Fall* (McGovern Award, Ashland Poetry Press, 2006), and *The Bodies We Were Loaned* (The Word Works, 2002), as well as the chapbook *American Gothic, Take 2* (Finishing Line Press, 2009). Her work has appeared in *The Hudson Review*, *Ploughshares*, *Poetry*, *Poetry International*, *Notre Dame Review*, and *Crab Orchard Review*. Over twenty-five anthologies have included her poems. She is the recipient of the Willow Award for Poetry, the Elinor Benedict Poetry Prize from *Passages North*, the Allen Tate Memorial Award from *Wind*, and an Individual Artist award from the Queens Council on the Arts.

Laura Tohe, a poet, writer, and librettist, is the Navajo Nation Poet Laureate and the author of *No Parole Today*; *Tseyi, Deep in the Rock*; *Code Talker Stories*; and the chapbook *Making Friends with Water*. She is also the co-editor of *Sister Nations: Native American Women Writers on Community*. Tohe's work has been published in *Ploughshares*, *New Letters*, *Cream City Review*, *Red Ink*, and *World Literature Today*, and has appeared in the US, Canada, South America, and Europe in French, Dutch, and Italian translations. Tohe is Professor Emeritus with Exemplar Distinction in the English Department at Arizona State University and is an Arizona Speaks presenter for the Arizona Humanities, which awarded her the 2006 Dan Schilling Public Scholar Award. Additional honors include a 2020 Academy of American Poets Laureate Fellowship and the 2019 American Indian Festival of Words Writers Award.

Natasha Trethewey is the author of *Monument: Poems New and Selected* (Houghton Mifflin, 2018), which was longlisted for the 2018 National Book Award in Poetry; *Thrall* (Houghton Mifflin, 2012); *Native Guard* (Houghton Mifflin, 2006), which received the Pulitzer Prize for Poetry; and *Bellocq's Ophelia* (Graywolf Press, 2002). Her first collection of poetry, *Domestic Work* (Graywolf Press, 2000), was the winner of the Cave Canem Poetry Prize for the best first book by an African American poet and won both the 2001 Mississippi Institute of Arts and Letters Book Prize and the 2001 Lillian Smith Award for Poetry. In 2012, Trethewey was named the state Poet Laureate of Mississippi and was named by the Library of Congress as the 19th US Poet Laureate. She was elected a Chancellor of the Academy of American Poets in 2019. She is the Board of Trustees Professor of English at Northwestern University in Evanston, Illinois.

George Wallace is the author of thirty-six books and chapbooks of poetry published in the US, the UK, Macedonia, and Italy. Recent books include *I Feed the Flames and the Flames Feed Me* (Local Gems Press, 2019), *Sacred Language of Wine and Bread* (La Finestra Editrice, 2019), and *Smashing Rock and Straight as Razors* (Blue Light Press, 2017). He is Writer-in-Residence at the Walt Whitman Birthplace and the first Poet Laureate of Suffolk County, Long Island. Wallace is the editor of *Poetrybay.com*, co-editor of *Great Weather for Media*, and editor of *Long Island Quarterly* and Walt's Corner, a weekly poetry column in *The Long Islander*. His poems have appeared in *Big Bridge*, *Cortland Review*, *Poetry Pacific*, *Sensitive Skin Magazine*, *South Florida Poetry Journal*, and *The Nervous Breakdown*, and have been widely anthologized. Among his awards are the Corona d'oro (Korca Literary Festival, 2019), the Orpheus Prize (Orpheus Festival), and the 2017 Blue Light Book Award.

Michael Waters is the author of numerous poetry collections, including *Caw* (BOA Editions, 2020), *The Dean of Discipline* (University of Pittsburgh Press, 2018), and the co-edited anthologies *Border Lines* (Knopf, 2020), *Reel Verse* (Knopf, 2019), and *Contemporary American Poetry* (Houghton Mifflin, 2006). His poems have appeared in *Poetry*, *The Paris Review*, *The Yale Review*, *Kenyon Review*, and *American Poetry Review*. The recipient of five Pushcart Prizes and Guggenheim, Fulbright, NEA, and NJ State Council on the Arts Fellowships, Waters lives in Ocean, NJ.

Marjory Wentworth is the author of *Out of Wonder, Poems Celebrating Poets* (with Kwame Alexander and Chris Colderley). She is the co-writer of *We Are Charleston, Tragedy and Triumph at Mother Emanuel*, with Herb Frazier and Dr. Bernard Powers, and *Taking a Stand, The Evolution of Human Rights*, with Juan E. Mendez. She is the co-editor with Kwame Dawes of *Seeking, Poetry and Prose inspired by the Art of Jonathan Green* and the author of the prizewinning children's story *Shackles*. Her books of poetry include *Noticing Eden, Despite Gravity, The Endless Repetition of an Ordinary Miracle*, and *New and Selected Poems*. Her poems have received seven Pushcart Prize nominations. She served as the Poet Laureate of South Carolina from 2003–2020. Wentworth is on the Board of Advisors at The Global Social Justice Practice Academy, and she is a 2020 National Coalition Against Censorship (NCAC) Free Speech Is for Me Advocate. She teaches courses in writing, poetry, social justice, and banned books at The College of Charleston.

Lesley Wheeler's new books are *The State She's In,* her fifth poetry collection, and *Unbecoming,* her first novel. Her collection of hybrid essays, *Poetry's Possible Worlds,* appeared in November 2021. Previous books include *Radioland; Heterotopia,* which won the Barrow Street Press Poetry Prize; and the scholarly study *Voicing American Poetry: Sound and Performance from the 1920s to the Present.* Wheeler's poems and essays appear in such journals as *Kenyon Review, Poetry, Ecotone, American Poetry Review,* and *Massachusetts Review*; and she has held fellowships from Fulbright New Zealand and the National Endowment for the Humanities. In 2011, she received an Outstanding Faculty Award from the State Council for Higher Education in Virginia. Poetry Editor of *Shenandoah,* she lives in Lexington, Virginia.

Catherine Woodard wrote *Opening the Mouth of the Dead,* published in paperback and in a limited-edition book art version by lone goose press. She helped return Poetry in Motion to NYC subways and is a board member of the Poetry Society of America. Her poems have appeared in literary journals, anthologies, and CNN online. Woodard co-edited *Still Against War / Poems for Marie Ponsot* and has been featured on the Best American Poetry blog. Residencies include Playa, Ragdale, Vermont Studio Center, the Virginia Center for the Creative Arts, and the Hambidge Center for Creative Arts and Sciences. She received awards from *Women's Voices for Change, Unshod Quills,* and *Willow Review.* She swerved to poetry after an award-winning career in journalism. Woodard is a member of the National Leadership Council of the News Literacy Project.

Kevin Young is the director of the Smithsonian's National Museum of African American History and Culture and poetry editor of the *New Yorker.* From 2016–2020, he served as the director of the New York Public Library's Schomburg Center for Research in Black Culture. He is the author of thirteen books of poetry and prose, most recently *Brown* (Knopf, 2018) and *Blue Laws: Selected & Uncollected Poems 1995–2015* (Knopf, 2016), which was longlisted for the National Book Award; and *Book of Hours* (Knopf, 2014), a finalist for the Kingsley Tufts Poetry Award and winner of the Lenore Marshall Prize for Poetry from the Academy of American Poets. His collection *Jelly Roll: a blues* (Knopf, 2003) was a finalist for both the National Book Award and the Los Angeles Times Book Prize. He is a member of the American Academy of Arts and Sciences, was named a Chancellor of the Academy of American Poets in 2020, and was inducted into the Academy of Arts and Letters in 2021.

Yvonne (aka Yvonne Chism-Peace) was the first poetry editor at the feminist magazines *Ms.* and *Aphra.* Recent work appears in the anthologies *Black in the Middle: An Anthology of the Black Midwest* (Belt Publishing), *Home: An Anthology* (Flexible Press), and *Is It Hot in Here Or Is It Just Me?* She has recent poems in *Bosque, Burningword Literary Journal, Callaloo, Contemporary Verse 2: Canadian Poetry, Dappled Things, Foreign Literary Journal, Geez: Bone & Breath, Obsidian, New York Quarterly, Pennsylvania English, Yellow Arrow Journal,* and *Quiet Diamonds.* Early work appeared in *161 One-Minute Monologues from Literature* (Smith & Kraus); *This Sporting Life* (Milkweed); *Bless Me, Father: Stories of a Catholic Childhood* (Plume); *Catholic Girls* (Plume/Penguin); *Tangled Vines* (HBJ): *Celebrations: A New Anthology of Black American Poetry* (Follett); *The Third Woman* (Houghton Mifflin); and *We Become New* (Bantam). She has received two NEA grants, a BRIO award, a Leeway Foundation Award for fiction, and a Pushcart Prize, as well as a Mary Roberts Rinehart fellowship and a New York State Council on the Arts fellowship. Website: www.iwilla.com.

ACKNOWLEDGMENTS

This book took time to bring to fruition, and we would like to express gratitude to a number of contributors who brought their enthusiasm and talents to the enterprise.

Our deepest, most heartfelt thanks to Cave Moon Press's Editor-in-Chief and Publisher Doug Johnson, who had the inspiration, fortitude, and goodness of heart to conceive and undertake this project, as well as the flexibility to revisit its direction and expand its range over time. We are grateful, as well, for Doug's work through the early stages of the design process.

Many thanks to Mark E. Cull for his superb design work throughout.

We'd also like to thank Sally Dawidoff for her ideas about the manuscript, and in particular, for her keen editorial eye with regard to the open call submissions.

Special thanks to the many wonderful poets who graciously responded to our solicitation letters and selected or helped select from among their poems the pieces best suited to this project.

And thanks to Fred Courtright for his work securing the requisite permissions.

Grateful acknowledgement to the editors of all the journals and publications in which a number of these poems previously appeared, sometimes in earlier versions:

KIM ADDONIZIO: "Creased Map of the Underworld" from *My Black Angel: Blues Poems & Portraits*. Copyright © 2016 by Kim Addonizio. Reprinted by permission of Stephen F. Austin State University Press. "High Desert, New Mexico" also in *Now We're Getting Somewhere*, W.W. Norton, 2021. Copyright © 2021 by Kim Addonizio. Used by permission of the author.

CAROL ALEXANDER: "Shadows That Are" originally published in *The High Window*, Issue 7, Fall 2017. Collected in *Environments,* Dos Madres Press, 2018. Copyright © 2018 by Carol Alexander. "Blue Calling" originally published in *Terrain.org,* 2020. Copyright © 2020 by Carol Alexander. Both reprinted by permission of the author.

ELIZABETH ALEXANDER: "Amistad" and "Blues" from *Crave Radiance: New and Selected Poems 1990–2010*. Copyright © 2005, 2008 by Elizabeth Alexander.

About the Editors

Carol Alexander earned her PhD in American Literature from Columbia University. Since then, she has worked in the field of education, first as a university lecturer, then as a writer and editor specializing in educational publishing. She is the author of the poetry collections *Fever and Bone* (Dos Madres Press, 2021), *Environments* (Dos Madres Press, 2018), and *Habitat Lost* (Cave Moon Press, 2017). Alexander's poems appear in a variety of anthologies and in journals such as *The American Journal of Poetry*, *The Canary*, *The Common*, *Caesura*, *Cumberland River Review*, *Denver Quarterly*, *Hamilton Stone Review*, *Matter*, *Mobius*, *One*, *Pangyrus*, *Pif*, *Ruminate*, *The Seattle Review of Books*, *Southern Humanities Review*, *South Florida Poetry Journal*, *Sweet Tree Review*, *Terrain.org* and *Third Wednesday*. Alexander's work has also appeared in English, Irish, Australian, and Canadian journals and anthologies. She has twice been nominated for a Pushcart Prize. Her work has been read on NPR and featured in readings throughout New York City. In addition to poetry, Alexander has authored children's fiction and nonfiction. As a freelance editor, she helps academic writers hone their work for publication. Her interests include psychology, environmental science, and film.

Stephen Massimilla is a poet, scholar, professor, and painter. His multi-genre *Cooking with the Muse* (Tupelo Press, 2016) won the Eric Hoffer Award, the National Indie Excellence Award, the Living Now Award, the IAN Book of the Year Award, and many others. His newest poetry collection, *Frank Dark* (Barrow Street Press, 2022), is forthcoming. Massimilla's previous books and awards include *The Plague Doctor in His Hull-Shaped Hat* (SFA Press Prize); *Forty Floors from Yesterday* (Bordighera Poetry Prize, CUNY); The Grolier Poetry Prize; the Van Rensselaer Prize, selected by Kenneth Koch; a Salmon Run National Poetry Book Award citation, selected by X.J. Kennedy; a scholarly study of myth in poetry; several Pushcart Prize nominations; and translations of longform works by Neruda and others. He has recent poems in *AGNI*, *American Literary Review*, *Barrow Street*, *Chelsea*, *Colorado Review*, *Denver Quarterly*, *Gulf Coast*, *The Literary Review*, *Poetry Daily*, *Poet Lore*, *Provincetown Arts*, *The Southern Review*, *Tampa Review*, *Verse Daily*, and hundreds of other journals and anthologies. Massimilla has exhibited his art widely and performed work at venues ranging from the Miami Book Fair to public television to Carnegie Hall. He holds an MFA and a PhD from Columbia University and teaches at Columbia University and The New School. Websites: www.stephenmassimilla.com and www.cookingwiththemuse.com

Made in the USA
Columbia, SC
23 March 2022

58008444R00174